HALL

of

FAITH

A Devotional Commentary

on Hebrews 11:1-12:3

Phil Corr

HALL OF FAITH

A Devotional Commentary on Hebrews 11:1-12:3

Most of the Scripture quotations, unless otherwise indicated, are
taken from the Message Bible, Copyright 1993 to 2002; and the
New International Version, Copyright 1984.

Nova Publishing
Bakersfield, California
www.novapublishing.org
Nova Publishing and the "*NOVA*" logo are service marks belonging to
Nova Publishing, Bakersfield, California

ISBN: 978-0-9981933-0-4

Manufactured in the U.S.A.

To: Professor Sadoughi
With deepest gratitude for
your kindness, academic rigor,
and Christian support of Sarah.
May you continue to live out
the definition of faith in
Hebrews 11:1 and to "fix your
eyes on Jesus the author
and finisher of your faith"!

Phil Corr's Published Writings

"The Field is the World" Proclaiming, Translating and Serving by the American Board of Commissioners for Foreign Missions

"Titus Coan: 'Apostle to the Sandwich Islands,'" chapter in *The Role of the American Board in the World*

"A History of Congregational Missions," chapter in *Modern Day Pilgrims*

Forthcoming Publications

"I Knew Jesus": A First Person Telling of the New Testament

Titus Coan: "Apostle to the Sandwich Islands

Hall of Faith

TABLE OF CONTENTS

ACKNOWLEDGMENTS

There are six churches to thank and many individuals. By God's grace, I have shared the Hall of Faith sermon series in some form to the following churches: St. John's (South Amherst) and Henrietta in Ohio; First Congregational Church of Eaton and Ault in Colorado; First Congregational Church of Charles City, Iowa; the Evangelical Free Church of Charles City; and the Church of the Living Savior in McFarland, California.

I first developed and preached this series to the yoked parish in Ohio during the 1980's. John Romelfanger was a member of St. John's. He gave me the idea for the series in 1984 or 1985 by mentioning how he could relate to the struggles of such Old Testament people as Moses. At that time I made a mental note to do a series on some Old Testament figures.

Thanks go also to Dr. Jack Allsop for graciously providing a place for me to do preliminary work on the series. The floor above his office in Amherst, Ohio, was away from the phone and other distractions. I hand wrote some material and typed some on my manual Hermes 3000 typewriter.

During the late 1990's I shared this series with the good people of the Eaton/Ault church. I developed the series further and was able to add some more life application.

During the late 1990's I developed a friendship with the amazing John Fanella. A gifted teacher and preacher, John has publishing experience, is a wonderful husband and father, and is a great encouragement to me--both personally and in my writing projects.

In 2008, I preached through this series as a major contribution to the 150th anniversary celebration--Vision 150--at the Charles' City church. I thank the folks there for their encouragement and receptivity. Additionally, when my close friend Pastor Mike Downey had a medical issue, it was my privilege to share at least part of the series with the Evangelical Free Church of Charles Free

Church. I appreciate their kindness in letting me share with them and then walking around the corner to lead the service at the Congregational Church.

In 2016, I began preaching this series for the wonderful people at the Church of the Living Savior. They are an inspiration to me and have amazing stories of faith. At that church I learned (with the help of a 7th grader!) to prepare my own static power point slides to go with sermons. In the age of the internet, "googling," and digitization there is a wealth of public domain material to use.

So, this series has been preached at least once during each of four decades: the 1980's, the 1990's, the "ought's," and the teens! Developments have occurred in my life, leading to adjustments--I hope for the better--in the series.

While standing in line for ticket pick up at Dodger Stadium July 1, 2016, with my daughter Sarah, I got to talking with several people including Scott Brown. Once he learned I was a pastor he asked the question many pastors cannot resist, "Are you a writer?" When I told him I was, he shared about Nova Publishing, which he had co-founded with Jimmie D. Werther.

We got together for lunch the following week and he shared about the good path to publishing. By the grace of God, I had already transferred sermon texts to book chapters. After updating and editing the manuscript, it is now ready for publication. Many thanks to Scott for his making possible what I doubted (oh me of little faith?) would ever happen — the publication of *Hall of Faith*.

I would like to thank my wife Karin for her love, encouragement and understanding of her "sideways" hubby--who loves to write. She also provided a critical eye to the almost final manuscript. I would like to thank my children for who they are: Don the creative; Sarah the graceful; and Betsy the joyful! Thank you for your love.

PREFACE

You hold in your hands what I call a devotional commentary. This book is, first of all,

- Devotional -

in nature. I have not consulted all available commentaries. I have not paid much attention to textual criticism, authorship of the book, or other technical matters related to traditional commentaries. My purpose in writing this book is to encourage you in your walk with God. It is my prayer that God will deepen your relationship with Him and that He will strengthen your faith.

By journeying with the faithful people of the Old Testament, you in turn can be encouraged in your walk with God. You take comfort from knowing that they were not some kind of perfect plaster saints. Instead, they were human beings who were obedient and faithful to God. The Old Testament (and, for that matter, the New Testament) presents God's faithful people warts and all--making their obedience and faith all the more remarkable. You may well have heard the expression that God can do extraordinary things through ordinary people who obey Him faithfully.

During my third decade of preaching through Hebrews 11, another devotional tool has been provided. It is Eugene Peterson's rendering of the Bible in *The Message*. Peterson brings to bear both his pastoral experience and feel for the original Bible languages to provide a blend that is dynamic and enlightening when it comes to the biblical text and life in the twenty-first century. In most cases, I provide from *The Message* the relevant Hebrews verse(s) for each display or chapter.

This book is devotional. It also has elements of

- Commentary -

in it. I have thought about who the author might be. In 1977 I heard the President of what is now called Denver Seminary-- Vernon Grounds--share that the text clearly indicates that Paul did not write the letter. He did not suggest his candidate for authorship.

Since then I have pondered the possibilities. Some people suggested Priscilla (or Prisca) the wife of Aquila--tentmakers who worked with Paul, especially in Corinth (see Acts 18:1 and 1 Corinthians 16:19).

Priscilla might have had some input into the writing of Hebrews as she and Aquila worked with a brilliant scholar and orator that they took under their wing. Priscilla and Aquila also went to Ephesus where they met Apollos.

Apollos was from Alexandria, where the teachings of Plato were known. While the Book of Hebrews is rigorously Christian in its teachings, there are some neo-platonic overtones in it. Alexandria was the city of Philo--a Jewish teacher who brought Plato's teaching to bear on the Old Testament.

Hall of Faith is also a commentary because I have worked in the Greek of Hebrews and the Hebrew of the Old Testament stories to which the author refers. I have used word books lexicons, and, yes, some commentaries--especially two. These two *Books* are: A. W. Pink's *Commentary on Hebrews*. Though a 19th century work, Pink combines rigorous scholarship and lively illustrations.

The story for the other main book is a bit more intriguing. A watershed day came for me in the summer of 1987. I arrived in Grand Rapids, Michigan, for an Annual Meeting of the Conservative Congregational Christian Conference. I arrived early because I wanted to visit Kregel's bookstore.

Back then the basement of Kregel's was full of old books on Christian subjects. I was looking for Peakes' *Heroes and Martyrs of the Faith.* There were five copies! Like *Hall of Faith*, Peake's work is devotional in nature. When you see quotation marks in this book, they are either from Pink or Peake unless otherwise indicated.

Most of the chapters conclude with quotations from hymns used at the end of the corresponding sermon.

INTRODUCTION

On the same day--evening actually--that I bought a copy of Peake's book, I retired to my room and began to sketch something that had come to my mind: the structure and rooms of the Hall of Faith.

As you have probably surmised by now, the idea for a Hall of Faith is based on the NFL's Hall of Fame in Canton, Ohio.   The official website [2008] includes a discussion of what is "Inside the Hall."

This presentation indicates that the "hall represents its sport in a great many colorful and entertaining ways.   Visitors entering the museum are greeted by a seven-foot bronze statue of Jim Thorpe, considered a legend of pro football."

"After ascending a ramp to the second floor, guests learn about the first century of pro football in the *exhibition rotunda*. Memorabilia, video, and audio bring to life the development of the game from 1892 to 1992.   The next stop is the *Pro Football Today Exhibition Area* which pays tribute to the current 32 clubs and highlights recent record holders in the NFL.

"Perhaps the most emotional stop during a tour of the museum is the *Hall of Fame Gallery* which houses the bronze bust of each enshrinee.   Completion of the renovated gallery occurred in 2003 and offers visitors the opportunity to learn about each member of the Hall through touch screen kiosks that include bios, photos, and video on the inductees."

"Artifacts and photos on each of the Hall of Fame members are on display in the *Enshrinee Mementos Room*. The *Super Bowl Room* recaps the 41 Super Bowls played to date, exhibits the Super Bowl rings, and displays several pieces of memorabilia from the game as well as the entertainment that has helped shape the game into a global event."

"*Game Day Stadium*, a turntable theater featuring a 20' x 42' Cinemascope screen was a first in sports when built as part of the

Hall's massive expansion in 1995."

"As visitors leave the exhibit level of the Hall and return to the ground floor, they enter into an *interactive area* that includes a Teletrivia game, Call-the-Play-Theater, a throwing cage, Madden EA Sports video game display and other exhibits such as a display devoted to officiating."

As you read the above description, you no doubt made application to the Hall of Faith as found in Hebrews 11:1-12:3. In the Hall of Faith, there are exhibits, galleries, discussions of individuals, and so much more. This devotional commentary examines the "Great Cloud of Witnesses" (Hebrews 12:1) of the Old Testament to encourage the faithful of the present day. While the Hall of Fame focus is on a game and on the men who play it, the focus in this book is on God and the faith that individuals have in Him.

As I have sketched out the Hall of Faith over the years, I have made refinements. Because there are no sketches or other visual aids, you are invited to use your imagination!

If you have checked the Table of Contents, you will note that reference is made both to a verse or verses in Hebrews, as well as the matching passage in the Old Testament. In three cases, no correlating Old Testament passage is given. Conversely, in the Supplement to the Moses Wing, no verses are provided from Hebrews. This is because the two messages are related to the theme of faith in Moses' time, yet are not specifically mentioned in Hebrews 11.

As we continue in the Twenty-first Century, I believe there is a need in the Church of Jesus Christ for a book that focuses on Hebrews 11. This book is humbly offered for Christians as we approach the end of the second decade of the third millennium after Christ's birth (as Peake's was written at the end of the first decade of the twentieth century). May we be encouraged to put our faith to work, even as we "fix our eyes on Jesus, the author and perfecter of our faith."

FOYER

Containing Three Plaques

- Section 1 -

"Faith Is"

Now faith is being sure of what we hope for and certain of what we do not see.
Hebrews 11:1 The New International Version

and "Commendation"

This is what the ancients were commended for.
Hebrews 11:2 NIV

When you enter the foyer of the Hall of Faith, you see three plaques: "Faith Is…," "Commendation," and "Faith in the Creator." In this chapter I will focus on the first two plaques.

The Foyer emphasizes the basics of faith. The legendary Green Bay Packers' head coach Vince Lombardi is reported to have opened each preseason training camp by holding up a football in front of his players and saying, "This is a football!" In other words, no matter what had happened the previous season the team needed to return to the basics of the game of football.

Similarly, it is not enough to talk about football… or faith! Can you imagine what it would be like if people only talked about football? Big stadiums were built. Cheerleaders were secured. The fine points of the game were analyzed. Societies were organized around the world for the encouragement of playing football.

But imagine that football was never actually played. People might engage in pre-game warm ups, but never get onto the field to actually play the game.

That is ridiculous! Football is intended to be played. In August of 2016, new members were inducted into the Hall of Fame. The next day the annual "Hall of Fame Game" was scheduled to be played. But it was cancelled due to grass issues (the application of paint that congealed into a cement-like substance that would have injured the players)!

It is sad to write, but this condition all too often characterizes churches in the United States today. Hebrews 11 encourages us to be active Christians, to live what we say we believe, to put our faith into practice. In this Bible chapter we read of examples of human beings--people like you and I-who put to work their faith in the one true God.

All of the people mentioned in Hebrews 11 are in the Old Testament. I once had a church member tell me that he could identify with some of the characters in the Old Testament--their struggles, their failures, their lives.

Throughout this devotional commentary, we will draw inspiration and challenge from the men and women discussed in this chapter, as we flash back to their stories told in the Old Testament.

A confirmation student once asked me how I could spend so much time preaching through one chapter in the Bible. It is because it refers back to so many people and their stories in the Old Testament.

As we enter the Hall of Faith foyer — or lobby--we will have a time of definition and introduction. Faith is defined in verse one; while the faithful--those spiritual ancestors of Christian believers-- are generally introduced in verse two. First, faith is defined. Then we hear of faithful people who lived out the definition of faith: these people are approved---commended by God.

Faith is defined in Hebrews 11:1. Here is how *The Message* puts it: "The fundamental fact of existence is that this trust in God, this faith, is the firm foundation under everything that makes life worth living. It's our handle on what we can't see."

Let's consider what faith is *not*. The Christian faith is not blind. Our eyes are wide open to the mercies of God.

Christian faith is not merely listening, as in "I've heard a sermon today and therefore have faith."

Hebrews 4:2 sheds some light here. Referring to rebellious people it says, "We also have had the Gospel preached to us, just as they did; but the message they heard was of no value to them, because those who heard did not combine it with faith."

Hebrews 11:1 tells us what faith *is*. I like the translation that says, "Now faith is being sure of what we hope for and certain of what we do not see."

In order to better understand and apply this definition, I am going to look at it word by word, as well as look at one phrase.

Faith. The Greek-English dictionary speaks of trust, confidence, faith "in the active sense." Did you catch that? "The *active* sense." We are not to be spectators when it comes to faith. We are to be engaged, active participants.

In Hebrews 10 we read of the promise of faith and hear a warning against unbelief. "The future and what is hidden from view are here closely related." "Faith, whether natural or spiritual, is the belief of a testimony." Verse one describes how faith "operates and what it produces."

One of the first words in this operating definition of faith is

Assurance. That word may also be translated as confidence, conviction, and steadfastness. Faith is the confident assurance of the things of God for which we hope. "Faith provides a firm standing-ground while I await the fulfillment of god's promises." Next comes

Hope. Hope is involved with faith because we hope for

what we do not physically see.   Then there is this phrase:

"The certainty of what we do not see."   The word for certainty may also be translated proof, proving, or inner conviction about unseen things.   Is your faith proven?   Are you as convinced about the existence of God and His written Word--and your need to obey them--convinced as much as you are of the existence of anything or anyone else?

The proof is in the pudding--does your (or my!) daily life give evidence that faith determines your thought and action? Many people have observed that if you want to know what is important to a person--what his or her priorities are--the best indication is found in that person's check book and credit card receipts.

Picture this to help you understand the phrase "what we do not see."   Imagine two people standing on the deck of a cruise ship.   One person can only see water as far as the eye can see.   The other can describe in minute detail the appearance of another ship.

The one who can see so far is using a telescope!   In the same way, "Faith gives reality to the heart of things outside the range of our physical senses."   "Faith demonstrates to the eye of the mind the reality of those things [that] cannot be seen by the eye of the body."

Another way of looking at the operating definition of faith is in the context of ownership.   You could say that "faith is the title-deeds of things hoped for.   Thus, a person who has true faith possesses the title-deeds of eternal realities, and the conviction and proof that these realities, though unseen, can be a living and effective power in his life."

Some of the possessors of these title-deeds are spoken of generally in verse two, where we learn that this kind of faith is approved by God.   This is the "Commendation" plaque in the

Hall's Foyer.

The spiritual ancestors of true believers are commended for their faith. By the word "ancients" is meant those who lived in former times, in other words the Old Testament believers.

Verse two shows that the definition is to be understood in concrete fashion--not an abstract definition, but something acted upon.

The faithful are praised for operating on the basis of the definition of faith. This definition has been tested over and over again, and shown to be true.

The word for commendation is linked to the certainty of verse one. These people showed, they *proved* that their lives were ones of faith.

I hope that we will all "value a Christian not for his or her intellect, natural charms, or social position, but for faith, shown by an obedient walk and a godly life."

Before having an overview of Hebrews 11:1-12:3, we need to realize that the end of chapter ten really is where this section begins. In 10:38, the author of Hebrews "quotes that striking word from Habakkuk, 'The just shall live by faith.' That sentence really forms the text of which Hebrews 11 is the sermon. The central design of this chapter is to show the *patience* of those who, in former ages, endured by faith before they received the fulfillment of God's promises."

"In Hebrews 11 the writer brings forth examples in which faith had enabled individuals to perform very difficult duties, endure very severe trials, and obtain very important blessings."

Chapter eleven has two parts: the first is a general description of faith. That is found in verses one through four. The second part --which comprises the chapter--is an extended illustration or declaration of this faith definition. In other words, we see people putting their faith in God into action.

"Their faith consisted simply in taking God at His Word and directing their lives accordingly; things yet future so far as their experience went were thus present to faith, and things outwardly unseen were visible to the inward eye."

At the beginning of my sermon on this section, I throw a football to a teenager. Near the end of the message he throws it back to me. This reminds us that our faith must be active. Are you a spectator or a participant?

Throughout this book we will be examining faith. It all comes down to the One in Whom we place our faith--and that faith itself is a gift from God.

- Section 2 -

"Faith in the Creator"

By faith we understand that the universe was formed at God's command, so that what is seen was not made out of what was visible.
Hebrews 11:3 NIV

The National Football League announces its annual inductees on the day of the Super Bowl game. That further indicates the relationship between the Hall and playing the game.

Similarly, putting Christian faith into action is an integral part of the Christian life. Some years ago a video was made that ties together the Hall of Fame and the Hall of Faith. The title says "Athletes in Action presents: Spirit of the game." The subtitle reads, "Featuring Pro Football's heroes of faith." Christian football people are highlighted in the film that reaches out to fans with the Good News of Jesus and His love.

In this chapter of the Hall of Faith we look at the third and final plaque in the Foyer. It reads "Faith in the Creator." Hebrews 11:3 looks back to Genesis 1&2, as well as other places that God the Creator is discussed in the Bible.

In recent years the theory of Intelligent Design has received more attention. There is a video on the astronomical side of the subject entitled "The Privileged Planet." It shows everything that had to come together for Earth to be a habitable planet with humans.

I do not remember whether that movie quotes Albert Einstein (I think it does) on the subject of creation. But here is something of what I found on the subject--Einstein is "recorded as saying that a 'deeply emotional conviction of the presence of a superior reasoning power, which is revealed in the incomprehensible universe, forms my idea of God.'" The

Christian teacher Dr. Hugh Ross "claims that, despite not believing in the biblical God, 'Einstein held unswervingly, against enormous peer pressure, to belief in a creator.'"

Another significant development regarding faith in the Creator God is the 2004 book by Lee Strobel---*The Case for the Creator*. Strobel, who previously wrote *The Case for Christ*, calls chapter one "White-Coated Scientists versus black-robed preachers." Chapter three is called "Doubts about Darwinism."

Most of the chapters are interviews with various kinds of scientists. Beginning with chapter five, the first part of the title is "The Evidence of...." The rest of the titles are: Cosmology, Physics, Astronomy, Biochemistry, biological information, and consciousness.

Returning to the Hall of Faith foyer, verse three concludes the foyer plaques. It says, "By faith we understand that the universe was formed at God's command, so that what is seen was not made out of what was visible." As *The Message* puts it, "By faith, we see the world called into existence by God's Word, what we see created by what we don't see."

Faith is defined in verse one. The faithful are commended in verse two. Both the definition of faith and those who had faith are centered in faith in God, specifically God the Creator. Faith must have an object and the One in Whom we are to have our trust and confidence is revealed as the Creator.

First, there is faith. Verse three begins with the words "by faith." That is one of the most important phrases in Hebrews 11. If you take a look for yourself, you will see that the second through the seventh paragraphs begin with those words "by faith." Within those paragraphs the phrase is used three more times.

Look again at paragraphs nine through seventeen. They all begin with that phrase "by faith." Do you think the writer is trying to tell us something? I do.

He is emphasizing that those who truly follow the true God are those who live their lives *by faith* in the creating, redeeming, sustaining God. It is faith in action. The word "by" means here "by means of."

Understanding the phrase "by faith" is very important. So is understanding the interrelationship between faith and understanding. This is a faith that brings understanding.

Saint Augustine might have had Hebrews 11:3 in mind when he wrote, "I believe that I might understand." The Christian faith is not intellectually bankrupt. Being a Christian does not mean leaving our brains at the church door.

We are to think Christianly, to use our minds. God commands us to use our reason. As Deuteronomy 6:5 puts it, "'Love the LORD your God with all your heart and with all you soul and with all your mind.'" We want all of our thoughts to be captive to Christ, to be so consumed by Him and His written Word that our thoughts are His thoughts, that our hearts are inclined toward Him.

Faith enables us to perceive and gain insight. One area where it is important to have faith informing reason is the creation of the universe.

Hebrews 11:3 declares that the universe was formed at God's command. When I write the preceding words, some readers might be wondering about evolution. I realize that the subject of evolution and creation is touchy.

We do need to realize that evolution requires belief--or faith—at least as much as creation. Evolution is a theory, though it is often presented as an established fact.

Bo Kirkwood writes about this and other matters in *The Evolution Delusion: A Scientific Study of Creation and Evolution*. Among many other helpful subjects, he provides a discussion of entropy (the second law of thermodynamics), as well as Darwin's

9

theory of the origin of the species.

An argument is currently raging as to whether the view of creation may be taught in the public schools along with evolution. The American Civil Liberties Union is fighting against allowing creation being taught in schools.

Did you know that this is a one hundred and eighty degree opposite position from the ACLU's position during the Scopes trial of the 1920's? Back then their argument was that *both* theories should be taught in the schools. I ask only that the ACLU be consistent.

There is a book that has been a help to me on this subject. It is written by a scientist who is also a Christian. Written by L. Duane Thurman, It is called *How to Think About Evolution and Other Bible-Science Controversies*. After reading it, I realized that the title is misleading. It should be called *How to Think for Yourself about Evolution....*

That book shows there are certain points of agreement, such as devolution--or development--within species. And certain other genetic developments. It also points out that we all reach a point beyond which faith is required: be it in evolution and missing links, or the Creator God revealed in the Bible.

There is another writer named Schoepfle who claimed that there is evidence of a tree going back 7 million years. Schoepfle said, "'I don't know what Jerry Falwell and the creationists do with that.'"

Leaving aside Schoepfle's *ad hominem* attack, I wonder what Schoepfle would do with the discoveries made by the Hubble Telescope that is orbiting around earth.

Due to the Hubble Telescope, scientists in recent years have kept lowering their estimate as to how old (or young!) the universe is. Those who believe in the Creator are not hung up on dates. They are focused on the One Who is timeless. What matters is not *how* God created everything from nothing, but *Who* did this creation: God did the creating!

The writer of the Book of Hebrews proclaims that the universe was created by God's Word. The word translated "formed" could also be "prepared, made, created." It is used in a three-fold sense. "First, there is the essential and Personal Word, the eternal Son of God." That is, Jesus the Christ, Who is identified as the Word of God in John 1 and elsewhere.

"Second, there is the written, ever-living Word, the Holy Scriptures." I will come back to this usage as a basis of faith in the Creator God.

"Third, there is the Word of power or manifestations of the invincible will of God."

The third use of the phrase "the Word of God" is what is in view here. The writer is "thinking of the creative command 'Let there be light,' interpreting after the fashion of the Psalmist,

"' 'By the Word of Jehovah were the Heavens made,

And all the host of them by the breath of His mouth....

For He spoke, and it was done;

He commanded, and it stood fast.'"

A future example of God's Word of power is found in the words of Jesus in John 5:28&29, "'Do not be amazed at this, for a time is coming when all who are in their graves will hear his voice and come out--those who have done good will rise to live and those who have done evil will rise to be condemned." "The visible universe... was called into being by Divine power."

A little while back I indicated that I would return to the second meaning of the Word of God, namely the Bible--the Holy Scriptures. It is through the Bible, the written Word of God that we learn of, and have reason to believe in, the Creator God.

Moses, a man of God and man of faith, wrote the first five

11

books of the Bible, including Genesis with its creation account. The true creation story was passed on by word of mouth to the time of Moses. God directed Moses by His Holy Spirit in the writing of the written account.

If you wonder about similarities with the creation accounts of other religions, I can assure you that the differences are far more significant. The book of Genesis begins at the beginning of created things, then moves on to specific people.

That is the order followed by the writer of Hebrews 11. "The faith by which he accepted it is faith in the Divine revelation; the first chapter of Genesis is probably uppermost in his mind, since he is about to trace seven living examples of faith from the subsequent chapters of" Genesis, with Abel being the first.

Verse three of Hebrews 11 tells us the *Who*--God the Creator. It also tells us the *what*--Creation. It further spells out the *why*, or the result--what may be drawn from the Who and what, when it says, "So that what is seen was not made out of what is visible."

It is creation from nothing--*ex nihilo*--by the Creator God. How do we know God did this? "By faith, says our author."

With that we come full circle to the definition of faith in verse one. Do you remember the second half? "Being certain of what we *do not see*." Verse three is another illustration of his statement that faith is a conviction of things not seen.

You might be asking, "So what?" Some readers may already have been helped by a reasonable reinforcement of belief in creation--or should I say faith in the Creator God. That should be enough in and of itself.

But there is more that can be learned for our lives from Hebrews 11:3. "Since God created the universe out of nothing, how easily can he preserve and sustain us when there is not anything in sight! He who can call worlds into existence by the

Word of His power, can supply for the neediest of His creatures."

There is great comfort in that. What is your need? Is it physical? Emotional? Spiritual? Relational? Financial? Vocational? Put your trust in the Creator God and His Son Jesus Christ. He is able to carry you through. He is the Creator Whom we worship and bless.

During communion some churches say the Apostles' Creed. This fine distillation of the teachings of many of the New Testament writers (see R. C. Sproul's *Basic Training*) includes the phrase, "I believe in God... the Maker of Heaven and Earth."

As St. Francis wrote in his great creation hymn:

"Let all things their Creator bless,

And worship Him in humbleness,

O Praise Him, Alleluia!"

GENESIS CORRIDOR #1

- Section 3 -

Abel: "Faith Offering"

By an act of faith, Abel brought a better sacrifice to God than Cain. It was what he believed, not what he brought, that made the difference. That's what God noticed and approved as righteous. After all these centuries, that belief continues to catch our notice
Hebrews 11:4 The Message

In my youth I had the privilege and fun of playing Little League baseball. I remember vividly several of the games. I'll share two of them with you.

One of the memories is my being plowed over at home plate by a very big alleged twelve year old. As the catcher, I held on to the ball! Then I sat out the rest of the game (in the stands) due to a headache.

Another memory is when I was playing right field. A ball was hit into the short outfield--not too far behind first base. I ran forward, put my mitt down, and--whaddya know--the ball was in it!

On that day my father had been able to take off from his busy schedule as a doctor to make my game. When I made the catch he stood up on the bleacher, pumped his fist into the air and proclaimed, "That's my boy!"

That is one of my favorite memories of my father. He was proud of me. He thought I did a great job making that catch. Upon reflection, I realized that he might have seen a little bit of himself in me that day--someone who tries to do his best and occasionally succeeds at what he does.

There can be a down side, a dark side to children showing the traits of their parents. Sometimes there are flashes of anger. Sometimes there is willful disobedience.

We see these two sides reflected in Adam's first two sons. One reflects his positive relationship with God. The other exhibits his rebelliousness, his sin against God.

There is Abel, the person of faith who is commended in the Book of Hebrews. He lives for God. And there is Cain, whose most well-known phrase has become a byword for selfishness. Hebrews 11:4 focuses on Abel.

With Abel, we enter the second (and by far the largest) section of the Hall of Faith. After the Foyer with the three plaques, we begin to look at the lives of those who have lived by faith-- however imperfectly.

With Abel, we enter the first Genesis Corridor. Verses four through seven outline lives of faith, with Abel being the first. The rest of the chapter describes other achievements of faith.

We are told that Abel offers God a better sacrifice. We read in Genesis 4:4 that Abel's offering to God is from the firstborn of his flock. It is a faith offering.

Why is Abel's offering better than Cain's? God had made clear to Adam what an acceptable sacrifice was. Adam had passed this on to his sons.

The acceptable sacrifice is one that recognizes dependence upon God for all things--provision for food, forgiveness of sin, and life itself.

Cain refuses "to come with the acceptable sacrifice because he considered the confession of his need demeaning." "By a Divinely-given and Divinely-wrought faith, Abel offered to God a more excellent sacrifice than Cain."

Abel offers his sacrifice "by faith." You may recall that the phrase "by faith" is the most important one in Hebrews chapter eleven. By faith, Abel is commended as a righteous man. He is well spoken of, approved *by God.* May we seek our praise from God alone. It is God's honor that we are to strive for.

God commends Abel as a righteous person. Remember that his faith is a gift. So too is his righteousness--he is justified by faith. Abel, the faithful one, is obedient.

In that obedience he still speaks. By faith he still speaks, even though he is dead. As the King James Bible puts it, "Being dead yet he still speaketh." That is the phrase best known about Abel. May it be true of us instead of the words of Cain who asks, "'Am I my brother's keeper?'"

Cain knows from his father Adam and by his brother's example how he is to worship God. Instead, he engages in a series of wrong and harmful decisions leading to the abyss of murder.

"In Cain we behold the first hypocrite. He refuses to comply with the revealed will of God, yet cloaks his rebellion by coming before him as a worshipper."

Turning now to Genesis four, we see that Cain's first wrong response is anger. Anger is the wrong response so many times in life. Yes, there is a place for righteous anger because of a desire for justice for others. But too often we use anger instead of some kind of positive response.

In Genesis 4:5 we read that "Cain was very angry, and his face was downcast." He knows what he is supposed to do, but he is angry and depressed when God looks with favor on Abel's sacrifice. God does not ignore Cain's attitudes of anger and depression. God cares too much about Cain to leave him alone.

So we read that God warns Cain. God cares enough to confront him. God asks Cain direct questions. He has previously dealt in a similar way with Adam when he says, "Where are you? Who told you of this?"

He asks Cain, "Why are you angry? Why are you

downcast?"   Anger and depression often go together. Depression can be anger turned inward (it can also be due chemical imbalance or genetic, both of which can be helped by the triad of treatment: doctor, support group, and medication [as long as that medication does not lead to worse symptoms and behavior]).   This leads to despair and reckless, harmful actions if it is not checked.

God asks these questions for Cain's benefit.   God already knows the answer.

God's third question shows Cain that there is still opportunity for acceptance.   "'If you do what is right, will you not be accepted?'"   God provides Cain a door of opportunity, of acceptance, but Cain will refuse to walk through that door.'"

God makes clear to Cain the danger he faces: "If you do not do what is right, sin is crouching at your door; it desires to have you."   For us, this means that either Jesus is our Lord, or we are slaves to sin.   "If we would master sin, we must first be mastered by Him who first mastered it.   We must be the Master's."

Even in the midst of the warning, God indicates the right way: conquer sin instead of allowing it to conquer you.   Cain needs to be in control over sin rather than have sin controlling him.

That is possible only if he turns to God for help.   Instead, he turns to his own desires.   Christians need to allow the Holy Spirit to rule in their lives.

James 1 gives a vivid contrast and description of perseverance versus sinning.   "Blessed is the man who perseveres under trial, because when he has stood the test, he will receive the crown of life that God has promised to those who love him.

"When tempted, no one should say, 'God is tempting me.' For God cannot be tempted by evil, nor does he tempt anyone; but each one is tempted when, by his own evil desire, he is dragged away and enticed.   Then, after desire has conceived, it gives birth to sin; and sin, when it is full grown, gives birth to death."

This is all too true a description of Cain. Sin takes over, because Cain the hypocrite does not put his faith into action. Cain rebels against God, goes his own way and shows an even worse response than before. He engages in deception, which leads to murder. This is the first recorded "murder-one," murder in the first degree: pre-meditated murder.

This is followed by God's judgment and Cain's worst response. God asks Cain another question, "Where is Abel?" Genesis 4:9 indicates the descent into hell. First, Cain lies: "I don't know." Then he tries to sluff off responsibility with selfish words that have echoed through time, "Am I my brother's keeper?"

By his response, Cain shows that while Adam is his father by the flesh, the Devil is his spiritual father. Jesus says that the Devil "was a murderer from the beginning, not holding to the truth, for there is no truth in him."

God does not let Cain off the hook. God says, "What have you done? Listen! Your brother's blood cries out to me from the ground." God hears the cries of His people.

God speaks a curse upon Cain. The ground had been cursed because of Adam's sin. It will be even tougher for Cain: "When you work the ground, it will no longer yield its crop for you. You will be a restless wanderer on the earth."

The way of Cain is the way of life without godly purpose or direction. The way of Cain is the path of hypocrisy. The way of Cain is to be avoided by the people of God.

"If you are walking in Cain's way--if you have rejected the way of salvation provided for you through the blood of Christ, refusing to accept responsibility for our own state or the state of others--heed the warning of God and turn back while there is still time. Reject Cain's way. Take the way of Abel who, though he was killed, nevertheless had the testimony of God that he was righteous."

Cain and Abel. One lived for God. The other killed for himself. Fathers, think deeply and seriously about what you are passing on to your sons and daughters. Are there attitudes and behaviors that exhibit anger, greed, lust or hypocrisy?

Or, is there a yearning to please God, to show forth the fruit of the Holy Spirit--love, joy, peace, patience, kindness, goodness, faithfulness, gentleness and self-control?

It is not too late to turn from that which pulls you down, and to turn to God.

I do not know what your family life was like--if your family is or was a good example. Bad example, or mixed. Whatever it was, Christ is able to help you break old patterns and to live a new life for Him.

Just think how others will respond. Yes, there will be some who are upset because the status quo is no longer in effect. But others will rejoice to see Christ in you, the hope of glory. By God's grace, show yourself to be a son or daughter of God--and worship Christ the Lord.

"Take my life and let it be, consecrated, Lord to Thee."

- Section 4 -

Enoch: "Walking With God"

*By faith Enoch was taken from this life, so that he did not experience
death; he could not be found because God had taken him away.*
Hebrews 11:5a NIV

and "Pleasing God"

*For before [Enoch] was taken, he was commended as one who pleased
God. And without faith it is impossible to please God, because
anyone who comes to him must believe that he exists and that he
rewards those who earnestly seek him.*
Hebrews 11:5b&6 NIV

So far we have already been in the foyer of the Hall of Faith.
In the previous chapter we entered the first Genesis Corridor.
When one combines the Abraham wing and the other people
commended in the two corridors, there are six people from the
Book of Genesis in the Hall of Faith.

In this chapter we will consider Enoch. "In Abel we see
faithful worship, in Enoch faithful walk, in Noah faithful witness."
"Abel shows us *where* the life of faith begins; the example of Enoch
teaches of *what* the faith consists." The life of faith consists of
walking with God by faith.

In this chapter we are going to take a look at Enoch and the walk of
faith from three angles: being taken up to be with God;
consideration of the time when he was still on earth; and with
regard to the importance of walking with God. Also, with faith
Enoch pleased God.

We learn that Enoch was taken up by faith. You will recall
that the phrase "by faith" is the recurring theme of chapter eleven.
The author is encouraging the reader to live by faith, to walk by

faith.

Enoch, we are told, did not experience death. The writer is speaking of natural death. Enoch could not be found. He was on earth, then he was no longer on earth.

He was taken up by God. Two other ways the word for "taken up" could be used are "transported" and "translated." They are both helpful in explaining what an unusual experience is.

Enoch was transported, he was moved by God from one plane to another. In our Star Trek culture, we might say he was "beamed up"!

Translation also includes the idea of movement, shift. "'Translated' signifies to carry across, to bear up, to remove, to change from one place to another."

When you translate a message from one language to another, there is change---language is a significant part of one's world view. Enoch was translated from the finite world of the moment to the infinity of God.

Enoch is "an example of faith and obedience toward God, and therefore [he was] translated to heaven." Genesis 5:24 gives fuller meaning to the phrase we sometimes use when we talk about physical death: "God took him or her."

It is important to recognize that--in the case of Enoch--it was done *by God*. It was not done by Enoch or in Enoch's power or by virtue of his own faith. God "simply took him home to be with Himself. They had been out walking, and God simply said, 'Let's not go back to your place tonight. Why don't you just come home to me?' And so he did."

Why did God do this? Martin Luther says it is "to show that death is not the end but rather that there has been prepared and set aside for people another and also a better life than this present life which is full of so many misfortunes and evils."

The author of *Ninety Minutes in Heaven* says, "I didn't want to go back" to earth from heaven.

Enoch walked with God and then God took Him to be fully and completely with Him. Only one other person has had the same experience. That person was not Jesus. We know Jesus died a painful death and was resurrected and ascended. The only other person taken by God in this fashion was the prophet Elijah. You can read the spectacular story of Elijah going to heaven in 2 Kings 2.

Elijah is walking with his protégé Elisha east of the Jordan River. Elisha knows Elijah is leaving for good, but he is stunned when "as they were walking along and talking together, suddenly a chariot of fire and horses of fire appeared and separated the two of them, and Elijah went up to heaven in a whirlwind.'"

Others searched for Elijah, but could not find him. I do not know how Enoch was translated by God, but I think it may have been quieter than Elijah's experience. Enoch was taken up.

Let's back up and consider Enoch while he was still on earth. Hebrews 11:5 tells us that Enoch was well spoken of and pleasing to God.

He was well spoken of. He was viewed with approval, as was Abel in verse four.

Enoch was pleasing to God. The Ancients referred to in verse two were also commended for their faith. Able was commended as a righteous man.

Pleasing God "is the obvious culmination of the account of Enoch's life, for having walked with God and having thereby come to recognize sin as sin and to have turned from it, Enoch inevitably pleased God in what he did. What could be a better testimony for any human life? What could be a better achievement than to have it said that you or I pleased God?"

Pleasing God ran in Enoch's family. He was part of Seth's line, the line that more than any other, sought to walk in God's way.

St. Augustine traces the City of Man through Cain and the City of God through Seth. Enoch's father--Jared--was of Seth's line, and therefore so was Methuselah, who came after Enoch. And then Noah. And through Noah Abraham, until we come to Jesus.

But the New Testament is very clear that it is not *physical* ancestry that counts. While it is a great benefit to come from godly stock, each person is responsible before God--to please Him by living for Him.

And that is why we now turn to the importance of walking with God. We are not to get taken up with the taking up of Enoch and Elijah. "The bare fact that a man who walked this earth many years ago escaped death may astonish [us], but it supplies no practical help."

We need to focus on walking with God while on earth. That is what Enoch did. Enoch "walked with God in an age when practically no one else did. He is an example of faith when it stands alone."

Enoch walked with God. "This was no casual stroll. It was the walk of a life-time. Moreover, it was a walk and not a sprint." For the long haul you need a walk, and this is what Enoch did.

Medicine now recognizes that it is better for your health to walk than to jog.

"To 'walk with God' suggests a life surrendered to God, a life controlled by God, a life lived for God."

There are many references in Scripture to walking. It turns out that there are 362--just about enough for every day of the year.

Pictures related to walking are meant to instruct us, to teach us. The Book of Psalms begins by saying, "Blessed is the man who does not walk in the counsel of the wicked." Psalm 119:105 tells us, "Thy word is a lamp unto my feet and guide unto my path."

In the Book of Proverbs, Wisdom claims, "I guided you in the way of wisdom and lead you along the straight paths. When you walk, your steps will not be hampered; when you run you will not stumble."

Ephesians 2:10 can be translated in this way: "We are God's workmanship, created in Christ Jesus to do good works, which God prepared in advance for us *to walk into*."

In his first letter, John writes that "if anyone obeys His Word, God's love is truly made complete in Him. This is how we know we are in Him: whoever claims to live in Him must walk as Jesus did."

Jesus Himself has much to say and teach about walking. He says, "Enter through the narrow gate. For wide is the gate and broad is the road that leads to destruction, and many enter through it. But small is the gate and narrow the road that leads to life, and only a few find it."

Elsewhere Jesus says, "I am *the Way*, the Truth, and the Life." Jesus is the true path.

Walking with God. How are we to do it? James M. Boice provides three helpful suggestions. First, we are to walk *by faith* in God, not trusting to our own understanding but believing Him when He tells us what we should do and how to do it. Second Corinthians 5:7 states this when it says that we are to 'live by faith, not by sight.'"

"The second requirement for walking with God is *holiness*. God is holy, and those who would have fellowship with Him must be holy as well."

"Third, there must be agreement as to the direction we should go, and this means agreeing with God who has planned the way for us.... If Enoch walked with God, it was clearly because he was not fighting or resisting God, but was delighting to walk as God was directing him."

"We need people who will walk with God today. Not flashes-in-the-pan. Nor shooting stars who attract you more by their passing brilliance than by their substance. We need steady, faithful people who know God and are coming to know Him better day by day."

"When we walk with the Lord in the light of His Word,
what a glory He sheds on our way.
When we do His good will, He abides with us still."

All we need to do is trust and obey.

- Section 5 -

"Noah's Faith"

By faith, Noah built a ship in the middle of dry land. He was warned about something he couldn't see, and acted on what he was told. The result? His family was saved. His act of faith drew a sharp line between the evil of the unbelieving world and the rightness of the believing world. As a result, Noah became intimate with God.
Hebrews 11:7   The Message

Noah is one of the most familiar Bible characters.   He is portrayed in many children's Bibles.   At home we even have a Noah bath book--very appropriate with the water connection! Noah has received friendly, humorous treatment from a well known comedian.

In 2007 the movie Evan Almighty came out.   It is based on the Noah theme, complete with references to Genesis.

It is possible--on the surface--to be comfortable with Noah. His very name means comfort or rest.

But when we begin to look at the true Noah, the Noah of Scripture, we begin to become uncomfortable.   We do not want to look too close because we realize how far short we fall in faith and righteousness.

But for our own well-being, we need to *concentrate* on Noah and the lessons of life to be learned from him.   In this chapter I will focus on Noah primarily through the lens of the writer of Hebrews, though we will also consider the divinely inspired words of Moses, Peter and Jesus.

There is so much in the story of Noah that I could spend multiple chapters considering him.   But I will focus in this one chapter on how Noah built, condemned and inherited.

I will look first at the text, then apply each section directly to our lives.   Hebrews 11:7 tells us that

Noah built.   Noah did so for three reasons: because he was warned by God; because he believed God's warning; and because he feared God.

27

Noah built because he was warned by God. We receive warnings all the time. We see street signs that say "Lane ends, merge right." On packs of cigarettes we read that "smoking is hazardous to your health." We ignore such warnings at our peril. And, in football, there is the all important "two minute warning."

In the Bible, we are warned by God. It is God who warns Noah. Noah built because he believed God's warning; he believed in things not seen. Noah believed God--he trusted in the Lord. Noah is faith personified. He is a living example of the operative definition of faith found in verse one, which says in part, faith is certain of what we do not see.

Sometimes late at night I get a kick out of listening to replays of Art Bell's radio show. Called "Art Bell, somewhere in Time," there are some pretty way out people on that show.

One time I heard a 1997 show where a man predicted there would be a catastrophic event that would affect the face of the earth. Very few people would be able to live on the surface of the earth for an undetermined amount of time. When was the time frame for this to happen? 1999-2001! I chuckled because I heard it many years after the years of a fulfillment that never happened.

That man was certain of what he did not see. And he was *wrong*. Noah was certain of what he did not see and he was proved *right*.

Noah "proved his belief by action. It is one thing to have a mental certainty that some event is about to happen: it is quite another thing to submit our certainty to the practical test and to go on acting upon it for a long series of years."

Noah acts on the basis of the warning of the flood that he has not seen. Noah also builds the ark because he had holy fear.

It is healthy to have fear, awe, respect for the Holy God. It is a fear that *energizes* rather than *enervates*. It is a fear that takes God at His Word and acts upon this Word. "A reverential awe of God is a sure fruit of saving faith."

There is a great need for holy fear in our day: a fear of God that recognizes the holiness of God; and stimulates abiding holiness in our life. God will not be mocked. We will reap what we sow.

Noah--because of the warning he received and believed

with holy fear--built an ark. It is described in the book of Genesis and is re-enacted in the movie "Evan Almighty" (a sequel to "Bruce Almighty"). The Bible describes the enormous proportions of the ship. It is going to be quite an expedition.

Noah built the ark to save his family--literally--from the upcoming flood. Noah is also a picture for us, as Peter writes about in his first letter (3:30&21a) how "God waited patiently in the days of Noah while the ark was being built. In it only a few people, eight in all, were saved through water, and this water symbolizes baptism...."

The salvation of households is emphasized in the early church nowhere more clearly than in Philippi when Paul says in response to the man in charge of the jail, "Believe in the Lord Jesus and you will be saved--you and your household."

By faith, Noah built the ark. By his faith, **Noah condemned the world** by his words and his life. Peter tells us that Noah was a preacher of righteousness.

Noah also condemned the world without speaking a word: "by his own example, by his faith in God's warning, his reverential awe of God's holiness and justice, his implicit and unflagging obedience in preparing the ark, Noah 'condemned' the unbelieving, unconcerned, godless people all around him. One man is said to 'condemn' another when, by his godly action he shows what the other should do, and which by not doing it, his guilt is" made worse.

Noah condemned people because of his vision, his ability to see by faith what was coming. "The building of an ark far inland must have seemed an absurd procedure to his neighbors; but in the event his faith was vindicated and their unbelief was condemned: 'through his faith he put the whole world in the wrong.'"

Even though he was ridiculed for building the ark, Noah pressed on. We see something similar in the movie "Evan Almighty."

"The faith of Noah stood out in glaring contrast with the world's unbelief." Noah's "is a story of faithful endurance in the midst of great wickedness. [His is the] story of a solitary saint." But we are not to feel sorry for him, because by his faith

Noah became an heir. It is called here an "'inheritance,' to magnify the freeness of its tenure, to declare the certainty of it."

Noah became an heir of righteousness. He became a living witness to the truth of Scripture already cited in Hebrews 10:11, "My righteous one will live by faith." "Noah's righteousness was the product of his having found favor and is therefore the proof of that favor, not its ground."

It is righteousness that comes by faith. I turn now from a consideration of the text itself to an application of it in your life and mine. I will follow the same basic outline as above, and ask first,

Are you building? Are you participating with God in the growth of God's Kingdom? Jesus calls us to lay up treasures in heaven by loving and honoring Him, as well as loving others through service, sharing and warning.

Have you heard God's warning? There will be another day of judgment. This time there will be fire instead of water. Have you heeded the warning?

Is your faith operative? Are you living out the operative definition of faith found in Hebrews 11:1--"Faith is the assurance of things hoped for, the conviction of things not seen."

Or is your faith a non-operative display model? There is a true story of a man who bought some fire extinguishers. They were clearly marked "non-operative, display model." When the progressive sale reached 50%, he bought them. He thought, surely they must work. He bought them, under the signs that said "No refund."

The man took them home, proud of how much money he had saved. He showed them to his son, who pointed out the holes in the bottom!

He took them back to the store, where a gracious worker offered a refund. But he decided to keep them as a lesson to himself.

Too often, our faith is "non-operative, for display use only." Is your faith operative? Is it something in your life? Or having to do with your church? Or something else?

Do you have a holy fear of God? Do you recognize your need for personal holiness and how it affects the life of your church?

Sometimes there are discussions among pastors and members that basically say, "Preach whatever you want, but don't get personal. Don't bring the Bible's clear directives to bear on my life. Yes, the person sitting *next* to me should shape up, but not I!"

At Gordon-Conwell Theological Seminary, students were jokingly told how to point during sermons. We were to cock our wrist so the people in the pews thought we were pointing to the person next to them! And you might have heard the expression that when you point a finger at someone, you are pointing three back at yourself!

Have you boarded the ark of salvation provided by God? You are saved through belief in the work of Christ on the cross and of the Heavenly Father raising Jesus Christ from the dead.

I am not saying, "Flee to the hills." There is no refuge there. Your only hope is in God. Are you under the wrath or the mercy of God? Your spouse? Your children?

Evan Almighty gets his entire family (and others) on his "ark." Noah got his family on the ark.

Do you pray regularly for your family's salvation? Continuing with the parallel outline, are you--like Noah--

Condemning the world? I am *not* talking about a holier than thou attitude or a hypocritical pharisaic looking down the nose at other people.

Did you know that if you are living a godly life, a life that pleases God, that others will sense their condemnation?

I remember when my son was approximately one year old. He was in a high chair for a memorial service meal. With his innocent eyes he looked at a woman sitting across from him. She said, "I haven't done anything wrong! Why are you looking at me that way?" He did not say anything, but something stirred in her heart that caused her to be defensive.

People might react against you. If that is the case, you can realize that they are actually angry at God. Jesus basically tells his disciples the same thing in his Upper Room Discourse in the Gospel of John.

Are you verbally warning people? Have you ever heard of

Corrie ten Boom? She and the rest of her family were put into a Nazi prison camp for hiding Jews. All but Corrie died in those prison camps.

But Corrie got better rather than bitter. She devoted the rest of her life to traveling around the world and telling people about the Lord. You might have read her book called *Tramping for the Lord.*" "Tramp" here has to do with walking long distances.

She was one of the kindest people you will ever meet. But she also spoke the truth in love. She once wrote, "If I straighten the pictures on the walls of your home, I am committing no sin, am I? But suppose that your house were [on fire], and I still went calmly about straightening pictures, what would you say? Would you think me merely stupid or very wicked?... The world today is on fire. What are you doing to extinguish the fire?"

Are you warning people? Are you letting them know of what Paul writes in Romans 1:18, "The wrath of God is being revealed from heaven against all the godlessness and wickedness of men who suppress the truth by their wickedness."

Jesus warns that in the last days "because of the increase of wickedness, the love of most will grow cold, but he who stands firm to the end will be saved."

A. S. Peake has the following challenging words to say about the role of the church--words that we might not want to hear: "It is the mission of the church to condemn the world's insensibility. But our churches have too many in them who exhibit the same lack of moral seriousness. Few things are more ominous than widespread disbelief in the great principle of retribution."

Have you built for God? Have you warned people?

Have you **become an heir?** Are you not only seeking and building God's Kingdom, but seeking His righteousness as well? Remember that Jesus tells us in Matthew 6:33 to seek His Kingdom and righteousness before all else.

We all need to realize that we are not able to provide this righteousness for ourselves. It is *Christ's* righteousness that comes to you by faith.

The greatest question for each of us to settle is, 'Am I an

heir?'" To help us do so, I ask you to honestly answer this question, "'Have I the spirit of [an heir]? Is my main care to make sure that I have the birthright? Am I putting the claims of God and His righteousness above everything else?'"

In this chapter we have been considering Noah, whose name means comfort and rest. Perhaps the Holy Spirit has made you a bit *un*comfortable while reading this chapter. Do not ignore His prodding.

Instead, may you be like Noah who comforted himself in the assurance of what God is like. Noah rested in the truth of God's command and provision. May your faith be of the same quality as that of Noah, who proved his faith by his prompt obedience.

As you do so, may you know God's true and deep peace.

> "Like a river glorious, is God's perfect peace,
> Over all victorious, in its bright increase;
> Perfect, yet it floweth, fuller every day,
> Perfect, yet it growth, deeper all the way."

ABRAHAM WING

- Section 6 -

"Response of Faith"

By an act of faith, Abraham said yes to God's call to travel to an unknown place that would become his home. When he left he had no idea where he was going.
Hebrews 11:8 The Message

Have you ever attended a political debate--or, more likely, seen one on T.V.? I know, it can get rather boring. But at most of the debates--whichever party it is--the candidates speak and the audience---at least part of it--responds.

There is action or speech and there is response. On the game shows, the audience erupts when a contestant is told to, "Come on down!" Or, on the former "Deal or No Deal" there are at least two audiences--close family members; and the larger studio audience. There is action and response--deal or no deal.

This chapter's passage speaks of an audience of one. God summons one person--Abraham. Abraham responds, and the promise is given.

In Hebrews 11:8, we come to the Abraham Wing of the Hall of Faith. I am excited to welcome you to this wing. It is the largest room in the Hall, because Abraham takes up the most space in chapter eleven. Indeed, Abraham is appealed to many times throughout the Book of Hebrews.

We are introduced here to Abraham by viewing his response of faith. In verse eight--and referring back to Genesis 12--we hear the summons; see the response; and consider the promise. We will also examine the faith response that is needed today.

In order for there to be a response, there must be something or someone to respond to.   In this instance, the response is to

The Summons, the call given by God.   God's call is a summons. It is given directly to Abraham.   It is given without regard to age. Abraham was 75 when he left Haran.   God's call may come at any time in life.   The lady whose prairie rainbow painting once hung in my office started to come to church and read the Bible when she was in her 70's.

The content of the summons is a command to leave the homeland (meaning country); to leave kindred (the hometown folks).

The summons is a call to separation.   "The call of God is a separating one--from old standing and state, into a new one."

"The individual, internal and invincible call of God is an act of sovereign grace, accompanied by all-mighty power, quickening those who are dead in trespasses and sins, imparting to them spiritual life."

In verse 8, "The central thing referred to is the divine call of which Abraham was made the recipient."   We have heard the summons of God.   Let us now behold

The Response of Abraham.   Abraham is the responder.   "For the first time in Abraham's life, God became a living reality…. Further, he perceived that God was an all glorious being."

The nature of Abraham's response includes obedience, faith and movement.   First, there are obedience and faith.   "Here is full obedience."   Based on Genesis 12:4&5, we can say that Abraham's obedience was immediate, thorough and influential."   It was immediate and thorough because "Abram went even as Jehovah had spoken to him."

His obedience was influential because Lot his nephew came with him.   His obedience was grounded in faith, as is seen by his movement.   It is helpful here to consider how far Abram moved in his *thinking.*   We are so used to thinking of Abraham as the father of the Israelites that we tend to forget that he was once a pagan in a pagan country.

Joshua 24:2 tells us that Abram's family served other gods. He did not come to believe in the one true living God on the basis of his own reasoning. God reveals Himself to Abraham. Stephen--the first Christian martyr--says in his last sermon in Acts 7:2, "The God of glory appeared to our Father Abraham, when he was in Mesopotamia."

"What marvelous grace! The God of glory condescended to draw near and reveal himself to one who was sunk in sin, immersed in idolatry, having no concern for the divine honor. There was nothing in Abraham to deserve God's notice, still less to merit his esteem."

A colossal shift takes place in Abraham's thinking. A major shift also occurs in his *behavior*, as is expressed by the actual physical movement of Abraham from Ur of the Chaldees all the way to Canaan.

Leaving one's home town, leaving one's state, leaving one's country to live somewhere else for the rest of one's life is a frightening thought to most people.

Some might welcome it as an escape, but once the newness wears off, it is the same old drudgery or worse, unless the person has gone in response to God's call.

I can understand any unease Abraham or you may have at the prospect of such an upheaval. While in elementary school, I remember being amazed at all the houses there were on the way to Los Angeles. There were so many people!

When I was a college freshman, I took a test that indicated I was the kind of person who did not much enjoy going to new places and meeting new people. Since then, I have: gone to the Orient, traveled around the world; studied on the east coast; taught a class in Indonesia; served on the West Coast, in Ohio, in Colorado, and

Iowa; and lived in all four of the continental U.S. time zones!

Abraham probably made some preparations before he left, but he could not check the internet for housing in the Promised Land. He could not pick up the phone and speak to Joe Canaanite about the lay of the land!

Abraham probably did make some preparations before he left. There is a need to avoid two extremes. We are not to drop everything (and everyone) and immediately go somewhere. The other extreme is to use preparations as an excuse to never go. As three men said to Jesus to weasel out of following Him, "Lord, I will follow you, but first...."

In the next chapter I will share with you about Abraham as the pilgrim of faith. The definition of a pilgrim is someone on the way from somewhere to some place else.

Abraham goes from Ur to Canaan. He does so because of **The Promise.** The promise is given by God to Abraham. Because it is God's promise, it is a certain, definite promise--"When God made His promise to Abraham [in Genesis 22], since there was no one greater for Him to swear by, He swore by Himself saying, 'I will surely bless you and give you many descendants.'"

In Genesis 12, the promise has to do with possessions of property and people. Canaan is the Promised Land, the place Abraham "would later receive as his inheritance."

The emphasis in Genesis 12:2 is on people: "I will make you into a great nation." Abraham would become the father of the Israelite nation. He is an ancestor of Jesus and is listed as such in the two genealogies given in the Gospels. God's promise of possessions is responded to by Abraham by faith. He went even though he did not know where he was going. He saw no real estate pictures. He had no guarantee other than God's Word.

"This demonstrates the reality and power of his faith--to leave a present possession for a future one."

Like Noah (as reported in the previous chapter), many of his neighbors probably called Abraham crazy. At least Noah claimed to know what was going to happen. Abraham does not even know where he is going!

Abraham and Noah have in common "implicit confidence in the One" who calls and summons. Abraham is walking by faith, not by sight. As Paul writes, "We live by faith, not by sight."

The summons has been made. The response accomplished. The promise made. We now consider

The Faith Response Needed Today.

We must -

Heed the summons of God's call. "The terms of the call which Abraham received from God are addressed to *our* hearts. A complete break from the old, [sinful] life is required of us."

As it was with Abraham, so it is sooner or later "in the personal experience of each of God's elect. In the midst of their worldliness, self-seeking and self-pleasing, one day He of whom they sought to dismiss from their thoughts, appears before their hearts--terrifying, awakening, and then attracting. Now they can say, 'My ears have heard of You but now my eyes have seen You.'"

"Has God become a living reality to you? Has He really drawn near to you, shown Himself in His awe-inspiring majesty, and had direct and personal dealing with you? Or do you know no more about Him than what others write and say of Him?

"This is a question of vital moment, for if He does not have personal dealings with you here in a way of grace, He will have personal dealings with you hereafter, in a way of justice and judgment. 'Seek the Lord while He may be found, call upon Him while He is near.'"

If you heed God's summons, you will

Respond with obedient faith. "Faith and obedience can

never be severed; as the sun and light, fire and heat." "Faith has not only to do with the grace of God, but with the duty of the creature." "Abraham's faith is hard to find these days."

But if we do have the faith of Abraham, we will

Claim the promises, realizing that in Christ they are now spiritual--not material promises of property. We are to be in possession of saving faith and share that faith with others.

The promises are given for us, yes, but not primarily for our private use. They are to be for the extension of God's Kingdom. God says to Abraham, "I will bless you.... And you will be a blessing."

Blessed to be a blessing by responding in faith to the call of God.

Have you heard God calling you? Is it to serve Him in another land? Is it to allow God to transform you in the midst of whatever your present situation or circumstance?

Responding in faith does not always involve moving physically. But it often means major changes or attitudes in you-- your outlook and dealing with situations. Seeing things from God's perspective. Responding in ways that are faithful to God and people.

Abraham's destination was Canaan. "Spiritually, Canaan foreshadows heaven. No rebel can enter heaven; one who is wrapped up in self cannot; no disobedient person will. Only those will partake of the heavenly 'inheritance' who are 'children of Abraham,' who may have his faith, follow his example, perform his works."

"Only one life; 'will soon be past;

Only what's done for Christ will last."

As you respond by faith, "be an Abraham and leave a mark on eternity."

- Section 7 -

"Pilgrim of Faith"

By an act of faith [Abraham] lived in the country promised him, lived as a stranger camping in tents. Isaac and Jacob did the same, living under the same promise. Abraham did it by keeping his eye on an unseen city with real, eternal foundations--the City designed and built by God.
Hebrews 11:9 & 10   The Message

I begin this chapter with a quotation from one of the all-time best sellers: "The pilgrims were clothed with such kind of raiment as was diverse from the raiment of any that traded in that fair. The people, therefore, of the fair made a great gazing upon them. Some said they were fools, some they were bedlams, and some they were outlandish men.... Few could understand what they said. They naturally spoke the language of Canaan, but they that kept the fair were the men of this world, so that, from one end of the fair to the other, they seemed barbarians each to each other.... But that which did not a little amuse the merchandizers was, that these pilgrims set very light by all their wares. They cared not so much as to look upon them, and if they called upon them to buy, they would put their fingers in their ears and cry, 'Turn away mine eyes from beholding vanity,' and look upwards, signifying their trade and traffic was in heaven."

Have you guessed the book? It is John Bunyan's *Pilgrim's Progress*. I begin with it because we are considering Abraham the pilgrim. Abraham is a pilgrim of faith.

In the previous chapter I defined a pilgrim as someone who is going from one place to another. A tourist is not a pilgrim, because a tourist returns home. A pilgrim is one who has left one place with the goal of arriving and *staying* at another place.

41

In Hebrews 11:9&10 we are informed that Abraham "was not to be at home in this world, even though he was called to live in it. From this time on he rightly saw himself as a pilgrim on earth and fixed his eyes on the heavenly city of God."

In this chapter we are continuing our tour of the Abraham wing of the Hall of Faith. In the previous chapter we looked at Abraham's response of faith. In this chapter we are looking at Abraham as pilgrim. As we look at these two verses ---as well as the Genesis passage--we will consider: the family of faithful pilgrims; and the city for pilgrims.

Verse nine mentions three people covering three generations, so I have given it the heading of the

Family of Faith Pilgrims. I begin with

Abraham. "Abraham is an example of how we are to be in this world and not of it.... He is an example of what it means to be a pilgrim."

That is why I quoted from *Pilgrim's Progress*, which contains Bunyan's "wonderful description of God's pilgrims. The scene is set in Vanity Fair, the author's symbol of the world and its allurements."

"Here are the three marks of the pilgrim: he wears different clothes, he speaks a different language, he holds different values."

The clothes mean "that the believer is clothed in Christ's righteousness rather than in his own self-righteousness."

A different language means "that the followers of Christ speak often of him and his concerns." By different values he means "that the world has lost its appeal for those whose eyes are set on God's glory."

Abraham was a pilgrim. To a great extent, for much of his life,

Lot was *not* a pilgrim. We met Abraham's nephew in the previous chapter. We see him again here in the decision over land in Genesis 13:1-18. Both men had become so wealthy that, in order to keep the peace, they needed to separate.

Abraham lets Lot choose, even though Abraham has the right to choose by virtue of his age and his relationship to Lot. But Abraham is a pilgrim who trusts God, so he says to Lot, "You decide."

By his decision, Lot indicates that he is a man of the world, not a man of God. He chooses what naturally looks like the best. But it is a bad choice. Surely he knows of the sinfulness of Sodom and Gomorrah. Eventually he will have to be rescued once by Abraham and another time by God.

There is one word that sums up the difference between Abraham the pilgrim and Lot the lover of this world. That word--found in Hebrews 11:9--is

Tents. In Abraham's case, his tent was the symbol of his pilgrimage, how he had left his comfortable home in Ur and would be a pilgrim throughout his life.

Lot lived in tents, too--for a while. We read in Genesis 13:13 that, after his decision, Lot "pitched his tents near Sodom."

And, despite the wickedness and great sinning against the Lord, Lot eventually moves into a house in Sodom itself.

By contrast, "the tent-life of the patriarchs demonstrated their pilgrim character: it showed their contentment to live on the surface of the earth, for a tent has no foundation, and can be pitched or struck at short-notice. They were sojourners here and just passing through this wilderness-scene without striking their roots into it."

In addition to Abraham, the Bible refers to two other patriarchs. They are

Isaac and Jacob. Abraham's son and grandson. They

are part of the family of pilgrims. They are, of course, biologically related to Abraham. But they are also called by God to be part of the household of faith. I will look at them in future chapters. These three, together with the others listed in Hebrews 11, were looking forward to the

City for Pilgrims.

Abraham was looking for a city with foundations, in contrast to tents that have no foundations. "In Bible days a city was a place of safety, being surrounded by strong and high walls: so in heaven we shall be eternally secure from sin and Satan, death and every enemy. A city is well stocked with provisions: so in heaven nothing will be lacking which is good and blessed."

I have just given away where the city for pilgrims is-- heaven. "It is the vision of the city of God that turned Abraham into a pilgrim."

It is the vision that makes other people pilgrims as well. "What is a pilgrim? Not someone who has merely left home. A person who has done that is a drifter. Rather, a pilgrim is one who has left home but is also traveling to another home. A pilgrim has had a vision of a goal, a destination, and is determined to hang loose on everything else until the achievement of that new and better place."

This city is spoken of again in verse 16 as the city prepared by God, for pilgrims--who are called aliens. Later in this book we will come to a further discussion of this when we look at verses 13 through 16.

For now, let's consider some of what all this means--or should mean--to us.

Were Abraham and his family the only pilgrims? No. As Bunyan "saw so clearly, this is the calling of any true child of God."

I have some questions to help you know whether you are a pilgrim.

Have you made the Christian faith your own, or are you just going through the motions? When it comes to baptism, there are two views: baptize babies or baptize people who understand what they are doing. The paedobaptists have Confirmation classes when the children reach Middle School. At that time they can make their faith their own. It is possible for those students or those who are of an age to request baptism to go through the motions. The important thing is to make the faith their own.

They or you may come from a godly family of pilgrims--and that is a wonderful blessing--but if you have not set out on the pilgrim road *yourself,* you are bound for trouble.

Remember Lot! Being Abraham's nephew was not enough. He made bad choices based on a human perspective, not God's.

The way to make the Christian faith your own is:

*Dig into the Bible, learn its guidelines for living.

*Pray--ask Jesus into your life if you have not done so already. Then ask for God's wisdom to live the pilgrim's life.

*Gather together with other pilgrims to study and pray, worship and praise.

The first question is, "Have you made the Christian faith your own?" The second is

Are your tent pegs loose?" That is, are you ready to continue in your pilgrimage at a moment's notice, or are you so comfortable that you do not want to budge? Here is a third question that kind of summarizes the first two:

Are you a pilgrim for Christ? I am afraid that many Christians are like Abram when he was in Haran, before he continued on his pilgrimage.

"You have been called by God. You have begun the Christian walk. But you have settled down in your Haran."

Unlike Bunyan's pilgrims, "You dress like the world. You talk like the world. You have the world's values. Tell me, those of you who live like this, how could anybody looking at you know you are a Christian?"

Be like Abraham was when he became God's obedient pilgrim. There is another thing to remember. You may recall form Genesis that Abraham built an altar.

This is not inconsistent with being God's pilgrim. Abraham's building an altar was a figurative way of claiming the place for God--"we are called to do that---*wherever* we are and at all times.

"We are called to be pilgrims, but that does not mean that we are to pass this world and leave it untouched. For the Master of the Heavenly City is the Master of this world too, and we are ambassadors of His Kingdom and are charged with proclaiming His rule, and actually establishing that rule, wherever our pilgrimage takes us.

"Do you live on this or that street? On this or that block? Then you must build your altar on that street and claim that neighborhood for Jesus."

I end this chapter as I began it, by sharing from *Pilgrim's Progress*. Pilgrims have come to the last barrier to the gate of the Heavenly City. That barrier is death, symbolized by the River Jordan.

Bunyan writes, "Now I further saw, that betwixt them and [the] gate was a river, and there was no bridge to go over; the river was very deep; at the sight therefore of this river the pilgrims were much stunned, but the men that went with them, said, you must go through or you cannot come at the Gate.

"The pilgrims then began to enquire if there was no other way to the gate; to which they answered, yes, but there hath not any save two, to wit, Enoch and Elijah, been permitted to tread that path since the foundation of the world, nor shall until the last trumpet shall sound. The pilgrims then, especially [the one named] Christian, began to despond in his mind, and looked this way and that, but no way could be found by them, by which they might escape the river.

"Then they asked the men if the waters were all of that depth? They said no; yet they could not help them in that case; for, said they, you shall find it deeper, or shallower, as you believe in the King of the place."

"When I tread the verge of Jordan,
Bid my anxious fears subside;
Death of death, and hell's destruction,
Land me safe on Canaan's side;
Songs of praises, songs of praises,
I will ever give to thee...."

- Section 8 -

"Child of Faith"

By faith, barren Sarah was able to become pregnant, old woman [that] she was at the time, because she believed the One who made a promise would do what he said. That's how it happened that from one man's dead and shriveled loins there are not people numbering into the millions.

Hebrews 11:11&12   The Message

Some years ago I received some news that made me chuckle.   I was informed that a relative of mine was going to have a baby.   Normally there is nothing funny about that, except for the joy of the news.   In this case, however, the relative had a grown daughter who was married and a child of her own!   That means that the son who was born is an uncle younger than his niece or nephew!

I jokingly suggested that the child to be born be named either Sarah or Isaac.   That is because the humor in that situation pales next to the story of Sarah and her son Isaac.   This borders on the miraculous.

In Hebrews 11:11 and 12, as well as Genesis 21:1-17, we see "the marvelous power of God-given faith to exercise itself in the presence of most discouraging circumstances, persevere in the most formidable obstacles, and trust God for that which to human reason seemed utterly impossible."

Verses 11 and 12 develop the promise given in Genesis 12. It is the working out of the promise: how and through whom Abraham would have countless descendants.

The first step in that promise is a son by Sarah.   It shows the importance of faith in the faithful God--the promise is fulfilled in God's way and in God's time.

These two verses "show what an intensely practical thing

49

faith is." They "demonstrate what great endings sometimes issue from small beginnings, and that like a stone thrown into a lake produces ever-enlarging circles on the rippling water, so faith issues in fruit [that] increases from generation to generation."

We will consider Sarah first, then Abraham, followed by God--mindful all the while of Isaac, the child of faith and of the operative nature of faith in our lives.

For faith, as we see in the life of Sarah, "is an intensely practical thing." She who had not been able to have children of her own now realizes the fulfillment of God's amazing promise.

On the one hand, the birth of Isaac is no laughing matter. Every birth needs to be handled in a conscientious way. How much more so with Sarah who is very much getting along in years.

Nevertheless, not long after the birth of Isaac, one can imagine Sarah saying, "'God has brought me laughter [she laughs], and everyone who hears about this will laugh with me.' [more laughter] Who would have said to Abraham that Sarah would nurse children. [Here she squeezes Isaac so hard that he cries, and she covers him with kisses.] Yet I have borne him a son in his old age.'" [She laughs again.]

This is a joke that everyone may enjoy. We do not laugh at Sarah, but *with* her.

"The laughter is believing, spontaneous and unrolled. For Isaac has been borne. The son of promise has been given."

"I am sure Abraham rejoiced too. But it is Sarah who properly leads the rejoicing. It was she who had been barren and who now, having at last conceived and given birth to Isaac, can hardly believe her good fortune or control her joy."

Do you know what the name "Isaac" means? "Laughter." It is still used as a name today. Some time ago, one of the leaders of the modern nation of Israel was named Yitzak Shamir. Yitzak is the more literal translation from the Hebrew of Isaac.

Isaac! Laughter! What a joke! How hilarious of God. It

is a good, wholesome, living joke.   Or, as we might say, "That's a good one."

Once again, this event does have its good serious side as well. That is found in the faith of Sarah.   It is the faith "exercised by a frail and aged woman, who at first was hindered and opposed by the workings of unbelief, but who in the end relied upon the truthfulness of God and rested upon His promise."

It is even possible that all of verses 11 and 12 are about Sarah and that this message should be called "Sarah's faith."

Look at the footnote in the NIV Bible at the bottom of the page.   It provides this possible translation, "By faith even Sarah, who was past age, was enabled to bear children because *she* considered God faithful who had made the promise."   [emphasis added]

With regard to Abraham and Sarah, "Observe what a blessing it is when a husband and wife are both partners of faith, when both in the same yoke draw one way.... It is a mighty encouragement when the constant companion of our lives is also a fellow in the same faith.   This should direct us in the matter of" choosing a husband or wife.

Sarah has reasons for rejoicing.   Abraham also may give thanks.   Even though I wrote that it is *possible* verses 11 and 12 referred entirely to Sarah, I think the weight of evidence points to Abraham.

He is the one who is enabled to become a father.   He is the one who, I am sure along with Sarah, considered God to be faithful.

He does so by faith, as verse 11 begins--along with so many other verses or paragraphs in this chapter.

What does Abraham trust God for?   The keeping of the promise.

The promise is one of having descendants.   Two similes are used: Abraham's posterity will be as numerous as the *stars* of heaven and the *sand* of the seashore.

This posterity--by the time of the New Testament--becomes one of spiritual children. That is what Paul develops in Romans 4:16-25. There are parallels between the birth of Isaac and rebirth as a Christian believer. Paul makes four main points about this in Romans 4.

First, "the birth of Isaac was humanly impossible." Likewise, it is impossible for us to save ourselves, to know the second birth of which Jesus speaks and Peter writes.

Second, "Abraham believed God's promise of a son because he was fully persuaded that God had power to do what he had promised." We too must believe "that God exists and that He rewards those who earnestly seek Him."

The third point is that it was done in this way to indicate that the glory is to be given to God and not to men and women.

Fourth, "Romans tells us that these events in the life of Abraham were not written for him alone. They were written for us so that we might believe and have the righteousness of God credited to us, as it was also credited to Abraham."

The letter to the Roman Christians, as well as the letter to the Hebrew Christians, emphasizes the faithfulness of God. With God, all things are possible. He is the one who does the enabling. He makes it happen.

God is the faithful promise keeper. He is "the one in whom we can have full confidence."

The faithful God fulfills His promise in His time, according to His timetable. God cannot be rushed. Nor will He be delayed. With that understood, we turn now to the

Application section of this chapter. Are you faced with some impossibilities? Remember Sarah and Abraham, who delighted in God and had faith.

Are you up against a situation that is insurmountable? Remember God Who is the faithful promise keeper. He is able to get you through. You can't, but God can!

Here are some of the **lessons** Abraham learned from their situation. The first lesson they learned is that *God is faithful and will keep His promise*. "Has God made a promise to you? If he has, you may be sure he will keep it…. The day will come when you will laugh with joy at the fulfillment."

Second, "Abraham and Sarah learned that *God is all powerful*. They learned that nothing is too hard for him…. God is sovereign, and he can do what he will in his universe."

"If God gives you a task, he will give you the strength and time you need to do it."

"A third lesson Abraham and Sarah learned, [is] that *God is in no hurry in carrying out his promises but rather [God] has set a time for*" the fulfillment of his promises to you. "One of the hardest things we face in life is what seems to us to be delays in God's actions. We pray. The answer is delayed.

"Then we fume and fret and sometimes set about to work out the answer for ourselves. What is wrong when we do this? Simply put: we are not trusting. We are doubting either God's ability to do what he has promised in God's timing. We need to trust God and wait upon him."

"The more the eleventh verse of Hebrews 11 is pondered, the more evident will it appear [that] the faith spoken of there is of a radically different order from that mental and theoretical faith of cozy-chair dreamers.

"The 'faith' of the vast majority of professing Christians is as different from that described in Hebrews 11 as darkness is from light….

"The one is inoperative and ineffectual, the other is active and powerful…. Is it not evident that the great difference between them is that one is merely natural, the other altogether supernatural?"

Isaac is the child of laughter, the child of faith. From Sarah and Abraham's "faith there issued Isaac, and from him, ultimately

Christ himself.

"And this is recorded for our instruction. Who can estimate the fruits of faith? Who can tell how many lives can be affected for good, even in generations yet to come, through your faith and my faith today!

"Oh, how the thought of this should stir us to cry more earnestly, 'Lord increase our faith' to the praise of the glory of" Your grace: Amen!

- Section 9 -

Reflection Seat: "City of Faithful for the Faithful"

*Each one of these people of faith died not yet having in hand
what was promised, but still believing. How did they do it?
They saw it way off in the distance, waved their greeting, and
accepted the fact that they were transients in this world. People
who live this way make it plain that they are looking for their
true home. If they were homesick for the old country, they
could have gone back any time they wanted. But they were
after a far better country than that--__heaven__ country. You can
see why God is so proud of them, and has a City waiting for
them.*
Hebrews 11:13-16   The Message

As we come to the reflection seat in the Abraham wing, I
have a question to ask you: Are you, like Abraham, a pilgrim?
You don't know? Perhaps I can be of help. In *Pilgrimage: A
Workbook on Christian Growth*, Richard Peace provides a
pilgrim/settler quiz.

Grab a pencil or a pen and answer these six (out of 23)
questions. Circle the choice that seems closest to your views.

1. Who do you pay attention to when they speak of Christian
things?

    A. A number of people.

    B. Several people.

    C. One person, mainly.

2. How do you feel when new people join your church?

    A. Excited.

    B. Glad but cautious.

    C. A bit uneasy.

3. Do you ever pay attention to a dream you have had?

    A. Yes.

    B. Rarely.

    C. Never.

4. When was the last conference or retreat you attended?

    A. Less than six months ago.

    B. Six months ago.

    C. Over a year ago.

5. Of the people you invite into your home, are they:

    A. From a variety of different backgrounds?

    B. Mostly Christian friends and occasionally others?

    C. Generally Christian friends?

6. In terms of your attitudes, do you consider yourself:

    A. Able to change some of these?

    B. Pretty stable?

    C. Growing more fixed?

As you look at what you have circled, were they mostly "A's," "B's," or "C's"? Or somewhere in between?

If you can picture a spectrum, a line with all A's on one side and C's on the other, you may begin to answer the question, "Am I a settler or a pilgrim"?

You have probably figured out that the A's are the pilgrim side and the C's are the settler side.

I recognize that this poll is partial and unscientific and does not adequately take into account your unique situation. Nevertheless, it is an indicator. If you are near the settler end of the scale, you need to start becoming sensitive to the boundaries of your life and how you are relating to them.

If you are near the pilgrim end of the scale, you will welcome the opportunity to gain some new insights for the next step in your journey.

That next step is to think about what it means to be a settler or a pilgrim. Peace writes that "the most important characteristic of a settler is that he or she has stopped moving; or at least he has limited his movements of growth to a fairly defined sphere. In other words, he has found a 'position' claimed it as his own, and settled down to live within its confines."

"I don't think most of us intend to become settlers. It is just that at some point we find ourselves in a really congenial atmosphere. We feel comfortable there. We fit. We are accepted. We share the group's beliefs, tastes, and ways of looking at the world. So we stop. Sure, we may not be learning much that is new nor having any particularly meaningful experience..., but by and large we are content.

"And it's easy to understand *why* we stop. There are many advantages to the life of a settler over a pilgrim. It's cold and dangerous out there in the world as a pilgrim. There is no telling who you might meet and how they might influence you. The world is a dangerous environment filled with wrong, even satanic ideas that do have power in and of themselves. Whereas in a secure environment, with well-defined and well-defended boundaries, there is a sort of peace.

"Boundaries are very important for the settler. They are the thing that gives shape and definition to his existence. They also define for him the people with whom he can safely associate, the ideas he can espouse, and the activities he can enjoy."

"A settler is an individual who, for one reason or another, has accepted a set of boundaries for his or her life that define and thus limit the nature and extent of his Christian growth. To be sure, there is some change, but it is always within fairly strict confines. Such growth is little more than pushing around the furniture of one's life from one spot to another. The dimensions of the room stay the same and pieces of furniture remain constant.

Perhaps "new arrangements of the furniture are tried out. But by and large, there is never any radical home improvement. Walls are never knocked out to expand the size of the place. New, large-size windows that let in lots of light just don't get put in.

"And heaven help anyone who suggests that the place could be improved by a new piece of furniture. The settler likes his place just the way it is. It's comfortable. It's predictable. It's a nice safe place to spend a whole lifetime. The trouble is, Jesus keeps talking about taking up crosses and bearing others' burdens and going into all the world, which is hard to do from your living room sofa."

Richard Peace--whom I knew while at Gordon-Conwell Seminary (I even square danced with his family!)--continues to write, "I have long been intrigued by the image of the pilgrim. For me, he has always been a tall, gaunt individual: weather-hardened, rugged, possessing only what he could carry in his back-pack. I see him on top of a ridge, resting on a wooden staff, looking out across the land with deep, penetrating eyes. He is a serious individual, interested only in what is real and true. He has little time for pretense. He is not, however without humor. In fact, his laugh is rich, deep and spontaneous." That description of a pilgrim reminds me of J. R. Tolkien's character named Gandalf in *The Lord of the Rings*.

This pilgrim "is on a journey. It is an important journey and one he has undertaken only after long and careful consideration. Now he is totally dedicated to it. He does not pursue his goal with frenzied haste. He moves deliberately and steadily, yet he seems to have ample time to enjoy what he encounters along the way--flowers, children, fresh grass, the sun, villagers, great libraries, and lonely caves.

"My pilgrim is a dedicated man. He has been called to persevere until he reaches his goal and he has willingly put all else aside to follow this solitary path. He knows he will not reach this goal quickly. In fact, he is on a pilgrimage that will take a lifetime. Yet there is no impatience in him. He simply keeps moving, encouraged by the sure sense that one day he will arrive and then he will find treasure beyond imagining...."

Learning is important to the pilgrim. It is "all-embracing, touching on every facet of his or her life--his mind, emotions, sensations, will, intuition, attitudes and his behavior. He wants to grow in understanding and wisdom. He wants to widen the range of his experience. He seeks to develop new and ever more healthy attitudes and emotions. He wants to sharpen his spiritual intuitions... He has no compulsion to know everything immediately, because he knows his learning will be a lifelong experience and he can afford patiently to pursue learning in depth."

The image of the Christian's life as a "Pilgrim's Progress is found throughout the Bible." "It is in the book of Hebrews that the concept is given its most complete expression." "This pilgrim image finds focus particularly in Hebrews 11:13-16."

This brings us to verse 13, which introduces pilgrimage. Verses 14-16 develop that theme.

Verse 13 looks back to people already mentioned in Hebrews 11, but especially to Abraham. We read that "Abraham obeyed, and thus Israel's history began as a pilgrimage."

Verse 13 reviews the promise. The Old Testament faithful did not receive the promise in the sense that its fulfillment did not take place while they were on earth. But they had excellent eyesight!

God granted them, by faith, the vision of the coming Savior in whom all God's promises would be fully met and realized.

The Old Testament pilgrims had great eyesight. They were kind of like the reports we have received about the incredible eyesight astronauts have returning from the Mir Space Station after months in space. They can see incredibly long distances and can penetrate obstacles, such as water.

As Christians think upon the realm of the Almighty, and fix their eyes upon Jesus, their spiritual eyesight greatly improves as does their ability to live each day. "The eye of faith is strong and endowed with long-distance vision."

Verse 13 refers to pilgrimage when it speaks of aliens and strangers. The Greek word for alien "was used for a person staying temporarily at a place but whose real home was elsewhere. To be an exile is a humiliating experience."

The Greek word for stranger is the word from which we get "xenophobic"--being fearful of strangers. "In the ancient world, foreigners and strangers were greeted with suspicion and contempt. When the tribe was all the security an individual had, he guarded it jealousy. Who knew why these aliens were really here? Perhaps they were spies? Foreigners were never really accepted into an alien culture."

"Canaan was for Abraham a land of sojourning and life for Jacob was time of pilgrimage." At the beginning of the Middle Ages, there was a devoted servant of Christ by the name of Basil. When he was threatened with exile by Modestus, he said, "I know no banishment, we have no abiding-place here in the world. I do not count this place mine, nor can I say the other is mine, rather all is God's whose stranger and Pilgrim I am."

Basil was a pilgrim, not a nomad. There is a difference between a nomad and a pilgrim. 'A nomad simply wanders. A pilgrim has a goal.'

That is something of Hebrews 11:13. Verses 14-17 tell of the pilgrim's goal, of Abraham's goal, of the Christian's goal.

Pilgrims provide a tip off of what they are up to. Verse 14 says, "People who say such things *show* that they are looking for a country of their own." "Heaven is here called a 'country' because of its largeness; it is a pleasant country, the land of uprightness, rest and joy."

Verse 15 indicates that they are not looking for the country they grew up in. For Abraham, home had been "Mesopotamia, the so-called cradle of civilization. Abraham did not leave the primitive backwaters to seek fame and fortune in rich lands. He left the heart of civilization to journey into the unknown."

For the Christian pilgrim, just as for Abraham, there is no turning back. As Jesus says, "No one, having put his hand to the plow who looks back is fit for the kingdom of God."

If we are not to go back, where then are we headed? Verse 16 tells us that we are to look for a better country, one superior to any place on earth. That is because it is God's country, heavenly in nature.

For the patriarchs, their true homeland was not on earth at all." "The earthly *Canaan* and the earthly Jerusalem were but temporary object-lessons pointing to the saints' everlasting rest, the well-founded city of God."

The great theologian Saint Augustine wrote a book called *The City of God.* The great eighteenth century Congregational Pastor Jonathan Edwards has words of exhortation to the Christian pilgrim on this point: "We ought to seek heaven by traveling in the way that leads [to it.] This is a way of holiness."

Again he says "we should travel on the way of obedience to all commands, even the difficult as well as the easy: denying all our sinful inclinations and interest."

The pilgrim's way is not easy, but it is much to be preferred to the other road that leads to destruction.

The pilgrim is looking for a country, a city prepared by God.

God prepares this city for those who obey him by walking in His way. God "honored their daring confidence by preparing" a city for them.

"The patriarchs honored God by putting their faith in him; he honored them by calling himself 'the God of Abraham, the God of Isaac, and the God of Jacob. What higher honor than this could be paid to any mortal?"

God identifies with those who have identified themselves with Him. The mutual identification will be full achieved in the city of the faithful prepared by God. As Henry Francis Lyte has written,

"It is not for me to be seeking bliss

And building my hopes in a region like this;

I look for a city which hands have not piled,

I pant for a country by sin undefiled."

Are you a settler or a pilgrim? If you are a pilgrim, you are homesick for heaven. "Heaven is our native land, and it is there only that the Spirit can be truly at home; but even now faith can enable us to enter in and breathe its atmosphere, since Jesus has dedicated for us the new and living way."

Are you a settler or a pilgrim? Maybe this question--and this chapter's message--have been **un**settling to you. I hope so! I hope you have been jostled out of complacency. I hope you have sensed a spark being kindled within you. May that spark become the pilgrim's flame, a torch to guide you on the pilgrim's way.

- Section 10 -

"Faith Sacrifice"

By faith, Abraham, at the time of testing, offered Isaac back to God. Acting in faith, he was as ready to return the promised son, his only son, as he had been to receive him--and this after he had already been told, 'Your descendants shall come from Isaac.' Abraham [reckoned] that if God wanted to, he could raise the dead. In a sense, that's what happened when he received Isaac back, alive from off the altar.
Hebrews 11:17-19   The Message

When I first preached on this passage, I could intellectually relate to Abraham because I am a father.   I could sympathize with his dilemma.   The second and following times I could *empathize* with Abraham.   I had experienced the geographic and relational loss of my son.

Sadly, I went through a divorce in 1992.   On April 15th of that year the court decided that my son would spend most of his time living approximately 20 miles from me.

In 1994 it was decided that he could go to another country. I was devastated again.   In the summer of 1995 I rejoiced (for his sake) that the court wanted him to live with me.

And then in early 1996 I learned that he wanted to go back to the other country because he had been told that he could attend an English speaking school.   I was ready to resume the court battle until my attorney said something like, "Phil, I can't imagine something that would make it worth putting him through another custody battle.   And, besides, at his age the court will let him do what he wants."

I later told my attorney that if God could speak in music through Mozart, I guessed that He could speak through a family law attorney! She got a chuckle out of that and asked me for permission to write about it in the family law journal.

But she was right. As hard and painful as it was, I decided, I voluntarily *chose* to give him up, to let him go--even though I had great concerns for him and sadness in my heart.

The point of what I am writing is that I have learned through my life experiences to identify a little bit with Abraham, to empathize with him.

You see, Abraham had a choice--to obey God or not. But the choice to obey God was a terrible one because it appeared that God was taking back His promise of descendants and blessing to the whole world. But Abraham chooses--in faith--to obey God.

I realize that the point of today's Bible story, the trial of Abraham's faith, rests on a question Abraham may well have had: "God told me Isaac is the seed of promise. Now He is asking me to sacrifice Him. How can I reconcile the divine command with the divine promise?"

As we shall see, there is an answer--both immediate and long term. In a little bit we will again consider the story itself. But first it needs to be said that "only occasionally does a story come along that is so unique that it captures the imaginations of people, not merely in one age, but in all ages. The historical record of Abraham's near sacrifice of Isaac is one of these stories. As F. B. Meyer wrote, 'So long as men live in the world, they will turn to this story with unwaning interest. There is only one scene in history by which it is surpassed: that where the Great Father gave His Isaac to a death from which there was no deliverance.'"

I turn now to a re-telling of the story found in Genesis 22. The story opens with a content father. Abraham has known the joy of the birth of Isaac, the son of promise. He has known the agony of ridicule and separation from Hagar and Ishmael. Now he is delighting to see Isaac grow in wisdom and stature.

Then one day God speaks, "Abraham!" Abraham shows his immediate availability by responding, "Here I am."

God gives Abraham a three-fold command:

*Take your son;

*Go where I tell you; and

*Sacrifice Isaac as a burnt offering.

We do not know what went through Abraham's mind. We *do* see his prompt, obedient response. Early the next morning he gets ready to go--he saddles his donkey, rounds up Isaac and two servants, and cuts enough wood for the burnt offering.

Then they set off for the place God had told him about, the region of Mount Moriah. After three days, Abraham sees the mountain in the distance. He leaves the servants behind with the donkey. Abraham indicates his faith in God when he tells the servants, "*We* will come back to you."

Then the long walk begins. Isaac is old enough and bright enough to figure something is missing. He speaks to his dad saying, "Father?" "Abraham again shows his availably--this time to his son--by saying, "Yes, my son?"

Isaac asks the big question, "The fire and wood are here. But where is the lamb for the burnt offering?"

Abraham's faith shines through when he says, "God Himself will provide the lamb for the burnt offering my son."

The walk continues--perhaps in silence--until they reach the top. Abraham builds the altar, arranges the wood, binds Isaac (who does not resist), and puts him on the wood.

Then Abraham takes the knife in hand. He lifts his hand and... God intervenes. An angel of the Lord calls out, "Abraham! Abraham!"

Abraham is available even at this point. He does not argue by following through on the initial command. Instead he stops what he is doing and says, "Here I am."

The angel--speaking on God's behalf--tells Abraham not to harm Isaac. He says, "Now I know that you fear God, because you have not withheld from me your son."

Next God does just what Abraham had believed he would. God provides the lamb for the offering. Abraham sees a ram whose horns are caught in a thicket. So Abraham offers the ram and names the place, "The Lord will provide."

Then the angel again speaks for the Lord and reiterates the promised blessing, "Through your offspring all nations on earth will be blessed, because you have obeyed me."

Then Abraham *and* Isaac return to their family. This story is explained for our benefit in Hebrews 11:17-19. As we come to the final and most wondrous display of the Abraham Wing in the Hall of Faith, we stand before it and ask how we may learn from it.

We learn, first of all, that it was done as a **test**. God was testing, not tempting, Abraham. The word used for test means to try, make trial of, put to the test. It is meant "in a good sense of God or Christ, who put people to the test so that they may approve themselves as true."

"It may be asked, 'But why should God try the faith of the patriarch in such a way?' It was for Abraham's own sake that he might better know the working of that grace which God had bestowed upon him. As the suspending of a heavy weight on a chain reveals either its weakness or its strength, so God places His people in different circumstances [that] show the state of their hearts--whether or not their trust is really in Him."

Abraham's faith is on trial as God commands Abraham to offer Isaac. Isaac! The one and only son by Sarah. The miracle child. The promised one who has brought such joy and laughter, as his name indicates.

Isaac is to be sacrificed. I come now to a problem that was

not a problem to the writer of Hebrews, nor to very many people until the 19th century.

"We need to dispose of a base charge that has been brought against God because of this story. For thousands of years, people viewed this passage with awesome respect and wonder. But in the nineteenth century the charge was made that since the passage tells how God told Abraham to offer up his son Isaac, and since human sacrifice is a detestable thing, Abraham saw God as essentially a pagan-deity who demanded blood sacrifice."

Such an interpretation goes against the clear meaning of the text. God is testing Abraham as well as anticipating Christ as our substitute. "The truth of the matter is that Abraham's near sacrifice of his son Isaac is pageant and prophecy of the actual sacrifice by God of His Son, the Lord Jesus Christ, on Calvary. It shows the love, not the cruelty of God."

I wrote above that the problem of human sacrifice did not enter the mind of the writer of the letter of Hebrews. I turn now to the **promise** found in this passage. "The ethical problem to which [the author] invites his readers' attention is this: the fulfillment of God's promise depended on Isaac's survival, if Isaac was to die, how could these promises be fulfilled?"

God had been very clear that Isaac was the promised offspring. "The impression we get from Genesis 22 is that Abraham treated it as God's problem; it was for God, and not for Abraham, to reconcile His promise and His command."

And God does just that by providing the substitute. After seeing Abraham's obedience, God reiterates His promise to Abraham, "I will surely bless you and make your descendants as numerous as the stars in the sky and as the sand on the seashore."

Rough estimates show that the number of stars in the universe and number of grains of sand are very close--both being about 10 to the 25th power!

The point is not that Abraham will literally have that exact amount. The point is that there will be many. A sub point is how remarkably accurate God's written Word is, that the two things are mentioned--stars and sand grains--are similar in number.

We have considered God's test of Abraham and God's promise to Abraham. We must not neglect **Abraham's faith**. Verse 17 tells us that Abraham did what he did *by faith*--he puts his faith into action. Abraham lived out the operative definition of faith found in verse one of chapter 11: "Faith is being sure of what we hope for and certain of what we do not see."

"What is faith? Faith is believing God and acting upon it. This is what Abraham did. God had shown that he could be trusted, so Abraham believed God and acted, even though he could not understand the solution to the difficulty."

Abraham's faith shows both hope and conviction. Hope that God would raise Isaac from the dead; and conviction that God would provide.

Abraham's faith is grounded in the certain hope that God could raise Isaac from the dead. Remember Genesis 22:5? "Abraham expected to come back with Isaac." This shows the extent of Abraham's faith, why he believed God--he believed God could raise people from the dead. Specifically, he believes God would raise up and restore Isaac.

The immediate object of Abraham's faith on this occasion was "the mighty power of God. He was fully assured that the Lord would seek a miracle rather than fail of His promise."

"Abraham had faith to expect a resurrection." Abraham had faith in the sufficiency of God. You and I know that God *is* able to raise people from the dead. We have the record of Jesus raising Lazarus and others. We have the history of God the Father raising Jesus.

Abraham did not have that benefit. But he shows such

faith! Abraham, as far as we know, had no precedents on which to base this belief.

What Abraham *did* know was the character of God--that He keeps His promises and that Isaac is the promised Son.

Abraham believed that God would provide. Abraham's faith is seen even here. When Isaac asks his dad where the sacrifice is, the substitute is not in sight. The phrase "God will provide" could also be translated, "God will see to it."

We have learned much from the story of Abraham and Isaac. Now I want to ask

How shall we then live?

What about our faith--is it like Abraham--who was available? Whose faith was active and long term? "We have to get it into our heads that as Christians we are into the Christian life for the long haul. For, what we need is commitment: to spouse, children, church, and, above all, God. We must accept a life time of discipleship. We must be pilgrims for God until we die."

What about your faith? Have you put it into action? Is it operative? Does your faith in God provide sure hope and conviction? Does it rest upon the promises of God?

Has your faith been put to the test in any way approaching that of Abraham's? Rather than considering what we may lose by putting our trust in God, let us consider what we shall gain. "The bounty of God should encourage us to surrender freely whatever He calls for, for none ever lose by giving up anything to God."

As I approach the conclusion of this chapter I would like to give you an update with regard to my son. We had the blessing of his living with us for his sixth and eighth grade years. In 2005 while at college over dinner he invited me to share my heart. He listened graciously as I shared with him the big picture and put things into context. As I write this he is living in a major U. S. city and keeps in touch via e-mail, text and phone calls. I would say that our relationship has mended. I feel that I have received back my son.

Returning to Abraham and the rest of us, we never lose by giving up anything to God, especially when we consider what God has given and provided for us. Isaac's substitute--the male lamb--was offered on Mount Moriah. One day that place would become the location for sacrifices in the temple.

And then, in the first century, Jesus--the perfect Lamb of God, our substitute--was taken outside the city wall to a place called Golgotha (Aramaic) or Calvary (Latin) or "the place of the skull."

Isaac, we are told, is a figure, a living parable--a picture foreshadowing what would happen to Christ.

Isaac was "only a test." Christ's sacrifice was the real thing. The cross is now the touchstone, the test for each of us. The test for us is whether we have accepted by faith this sacrifice for us. And, in Romans 12:1, Paul calls us to be "living sacrifices."

Christ was crucified. Are you following the crucified one? Do you take up the cross daily?

> "Crown Him with many crowns,
> The Lamb upon His throne....
> Crown Him the Lord of Love;
> Behold His hands and side,
> Rich wounds, yet visible above,
> In beauty glorified."

GENESIS CORRIDOR #2

"Faith at Death"

- Section 11 -

Isaac

By an act of faith, Isaac reached into the future as he blessed
Jacob and Esau.
Hebrews 11:20   The Message

In this chapter we enter the second Genesis Corridor. In this corridor we will consider Isaac, Jacob and Joseph. Instead of being near the beginning of book of Genesis, we are at the end of the first book of the Bible.

The writer of the letter to the Hebrew Christians relates the faith of these three men at the same point of life--near the end. Each one of these men--even with their all too human flaws--shows us how to "finish well."

Words of blessing and prophecy are spoken from the death bed, or soon before it. Today's passage speaks of Isaac blessing his two sons in regard to their future.

You might recall that the brothers Esau and Jacob did not get along very well. That is a bit of an understatement.

If ever there was a case of sibling rivalry, this is it! It showed itself the day these twins were born. Esau--named that because of his red hair--comes out of the womb first.

But the second one comes out grabbing his brother's heel. So he is named Jacob, meaning "grasper of the heel" and "deceiver."

Later on, Esau sells his birthright, his inheritance, for some beef stew when he returns hungry from the field.

There is at least one other thing that you should know before we come to the main Old Testament text for this chapter. That is, each parent has his or her favorite. Try as we might, most among us who have more than one child tend to have a favorite.

Jacob and Esau are a perhaps not so extreme example. Jacob is a mamma's boy, and Esau might be called a "man's man."

Rebekah, remembering the Lord's prophecy that the elder would serve the younger, favors Jacob. Isaac delights in the food Esau hunts and prepares. That leads us to Genesis 27, where Isaac asks Esau to do just that and receive his blessing.

The writer of Hebrews chooses one incident from Isaac's career as a token of his faith. That incident is his blessing Jacob and Esau.

Before proceeding further into this chapter, please note that most of the quotations are from James M. Boice's *Exegetical Commentary on Genesis*, volume two.

As we consider "the importance of this episode, we need to guard against two extremes: either to condemn the characters entirely, without any recognition of their motives, or to excuse them at the expense of true morality."

If we excuse them, "We may run the risk of compromising God's holy law." If we dismiss them out of hand, "We may thus strengthen in ourselves and others a prejudice, not only against the godly, but against their godliness itself."

"The truth of the matter, though we do not like to admit it, is that the characters are very much like ourselves. The point is that the sovereign will of God is done, in spite of our or any other person's opposition to it."

I am actually encouraged by this passage. It shows that God is able to work even in the midst of dysfunctional families.

In 2008 a movie came out that was called "Vantage Point." It shows the same event and subsequent developments from the perspective of different people. It starts at noon and re-sets at noon when the next vantage point is presented. In this chapter, I will look at the subject of faith blessing from the vantage points of the four very real characters in Genesis 27: Rebekah, Jacob, Esau, and Isaac. In other words--mom, the two sons, then dad.

First, let's consider **Rebekah**. She is Isaac's wife, as well as the mother of Jacob and Esau. "A home usually takes its chief characteristics from the mother, and in this case the friction and mood of distrust must be traced to Rebekah.

"Have you noticed how no one in this household trusted anyone else? Isaac did not trust his wife Rebekah, nor she her husband. Jacob knew that his father would not trust him ('What if my father touches me? I would appear to be tricking him.').

"Neither of the sons trusts the other. Where does this suspicion come from if not from Rebekah, who is seen here listening at the keyhole as Isaac and Esau talk? One commentator calls her 'a deceitful, proud selfish woman who wanted her way and not the Lord's.'"

Rebekah's real failure was *spiritual*. She was right in clinging to the promise of God and in perceiving that Isaac was willfully rejecting that promise in favor of the preferred son.

"But her fault lay in failing to trust God to bring the blessing to Jacob in his own time and way.... The dilemma Rebekah faced was of her own making, and the disposal of the blessing was God's affair and not hers. She had no right to do evil--and that of such a distasteful nature--that good might come.

"Having done it her way, good did not come." The price paid for the blessing "was twenty years of unexpected exile for Jacob, exile for which he had not been prepared by his sheltered life at home.

"If you are not trusting God and are therefore trying to do your will instead of His, or even His will in your own way, learn that the plottings of sin never work out and that the path of disobedience is always rocky…. It is better to wait for God at the beginning."

With that, we come to **Jacob**, who may well be the basest character in this episode. He is no child; he is a mature adult. "Yet, not only does he go along with Rebekah's scheming, but he adds to it by lying to his father and even dragging the name of God into his deception."

It is true that Isaac said that the other brother would call Jacob (whom he thought was Esau) his lord and would bow before him.

But again, there is a steep price to pay for deception. "Before Esau called Jacob his lord, Jacob thus saluted him. Before Esau ever bowed to Jacob, Jacob bowed low before Esau" when Jacob returned from twenty years of exile.

"Truly, the path of sin is hard, and the pleasure of sin is never worth the price that must be paid for it."

Jacob did **Esau** dirty--more than once. "It is easy to sympathize with Esau, as many have. True, he had tried to get the drop on Jacob by agreeing to his father's plan to bless him secretly; he had merely been outwitted by those shrewder than himself."

"But when we see him weeping aloud and crying pitifully, 'Do you have only one blessing my father? Bless me too, my father!' our hearts go out to him. We want to comfort him.

"It is not wise for us to do this, however. The reason is that this is not the way the Bible teaches us to regard the plight of Esau. What we are to learn and do is stated for us in Hebrews, from which so many other comments on the patriarchs have come.

"The author of Hebrews writes in chapter 12:5-7, 'See to it that no one misses the grace of God and that no bitter root grows up to cause trouble and defile many. See that no one is sexually immoral, or is godless like Esau, who for a single meal sold his inheritance rights as the oldest son. Afterward, as you know, when he wanted to inherit this blessing, he was rejected. He could bring about no change of mind, though he sought the blessing with tears.'

"In these verses God does not call upon us to sympathize with Esau but to learn from him, warning that although God is exceedingly gracious and is forever tempering justice with mercy, there are nevertheless choices in life that cannot be undone and consequences of sin that are thereafter unavoidable.

"If you reject the grace of God in Christ now, who knows whether you will ever again experience a spiritually melting heart and have an opportunity to turn to Him? If you reject the revealed Word of God in some matter and instead do what you know to be wrong, who knows whether you will ever have a chance to make that wrong right or avoid the destructive consequences that follow?"

In this case, "tears mean nothing. Esau wept, but his tears were of frustrated selfishness and not of genuine regret for wrongs committed. The only true repentance is a turning from sin to do what God desires."

One who came to a belated realization of what God desires is **Isaac**. He is the focus of Hebrews 11:20 As we look back to Genesis 27, Isaac does not begin this part of his life well. As a matter of fact, we would be well served to consider Isaac's entire life in context.

Pink writes, "Taking it on the whole, the life of Isaac is a disappointing one; it begins brightly, but ends amid the shadows-- like that of so many, it failed to fulfill its early promise."

One person has said "that old age can be a blessing or a horror." It seems to have been mostly the latter for Isaac. This is not a pretty picture.

Isaac is as scheming as Rebekah. He knows that God had

spoken of Jacob, but Isaac wants to put Esau first. He knows there would be an intolerable uproar in the house if he let out his idea. Boice writes, "Rebekah would protest and make Isaac's life miserable. To avoid this, Isaac decided to give the blessing secretly."

"Isaac's real problem was his defiance of the revealed will of God." He surely knows that the older would serve the younger. "He is like many in our day who think they can defy the almighty God successfully."

But Isaac does provide one bright spot in this otherwise drear family portrait. It is that spot which the Holy Spirit chooses to highlight in Hebrews 11:20.

That one act is found in Genesis 27:44. It "is a spot that stands out so brightly that one can end only by praise the wisdom and mercy of God, who brought it about."

What God brings about is a "conversion in Isaac from a willful rejection of the sovereign decree of God to an obedient acceptance of it."

"The blessing has been given. Jacob had returned to Rebekah, and Esau had appeared in the tent to offer the fruit of his hunting.

"'Who are you?' Isaac asks. When Esau replies, 'I am your son, your firstborn Esau,' the light begins to dawn within the soul of the blinded patriarch and, as the text says, 'Isaac trembled violently.'"

Boice explains this verse for us. "What was happening to Isaac? It was the realization that he had tried to box with God and had been defeated, and that he would always be defeated, unless he surrendered his own erring will to the Almighty."

Isaac's self-will can be compared "to a great edifice built in opposition to the revealed will of God. That edifice had to come down. Before God acted, that structure had seemed quite substantial. Isaac was not going to let it be shaken by that contentious wife of his, or that sniveling sissy, Jacob. But Isaac had failed to reckon with God -- God was out of the picture.

"Actually God was there all along. Isaac's schemes went awry, and he saw that in spite of his arrogance there was nevertheless a glorious, divine will above his own."

The breaking of Isaac's self-will comes almost immediately. "At the beginning of verse 33 the light dawns, and by the end of the verse the struggle is over. Isaac begins by saying, 'Who was it, then, that hunted game and brought it to me? I ate it just before you came and I blessed him.' He ends: 'And indeed *he will be blessed.'*

"'He... will... be... blessed.' Those words were torn from Isaac's heart by the most wrenching experience of his life. But though willful and late he had at last come out on the right side, and God never forgot that he had."

In the New International Version, you will notice a dash just before "and he will be blessed." I agree with Boice and other expositors who believe that God sovereignty revealed His will to Isaac during the pause that that dash represents.

"This is why, years later, when the letter to the Hebrews came to be written and the great eleventh chapter on the heroes of faith was composed, God made sure that it said, 'By faith Isaac blessed Jacob and Esau in regard to their future.'

"It is not much. Moses gets a paragraph of commendation [what I call a wing in the Hall of Faith]. Abraham gets a summation of the four central events in his distinguished life [in the largest wing of the hall].

"'By faith Isaac blessed Jacob' is enough, and it is significant that it is all praise and no criticism. Isaac fought God's will for many years. But once his own will was broken, God saw the new Isaac and remembered his sins against him no more. Oh, the

77

greatness of God!   Oh, the happiness of the one who is surrendered to Him!

"Are you surrendered to God?   Has your own selfish will been broken?   Before any great work of grace, there must be the internal earthquake [like] Isaac experienced.   If you are not God's, the earthquake must come and your own ways must crash to destruction before it."

In 2008 there was an earthquake in an unexpected location--southeastern Illinois.   I spoke with a friend in Evansville who definitely felt the quake!

God broke into Isaac's consciousness in mid-speech and revealed with His glory that Jacob was the one who was and would be blessed-- "He will be blessed!"

Spiritual earthquakes are unavoidable.   If you live in tornado country, you need a solid brick home or something similar. In earthquake country you want a strong yet flexible foundation with a wooden structure.

When it comes to spiritual earthquakes, will you be like a brick structure that crumbles during an earthquake; or a wooden structure that sways and survives?

Isaac spoke and held to a faith blessing.   Pink writes that "by faith Isaac blessed Jacob and Esau in regard to their future." This 'blessing was more than a dying father expressing good-will to his sons: it was extraordinary.   Isaac spoke as a prophet of God, announcing the future of his posterity and various portions each would receive.

"As the mouthpiece of the Lord, he did, by the spirit of prophecy, announce beforehand what should be the particular estate of his two sons; and so his words have been fulfilled."

Though parents today are not (often!) supernaturally gifted to foretell the future of their children, it is their duty and privilege to search the Bible and learn what promises God has put there for the righteous in Christ and their children," and to lay hold of these promises--these faith blessings--in prayer.

"Standing on the promises of Christ my King,
Through eternal ages let His praises ring,
Glory in the highest, I will shout and sing,
Standing on the promises of God."

- Section 12 -

Jacob: Blessing and Worshiping by Faith

By an act of faith, Jacob on his deathbed blessed each of Joseph's sons in turn, blessing them with God's blessing, not his own--as he bowed worshipfully upon his staff.
Hebrews 11:21   The Message

If you thought the previous chapter's family was in a sad state, wait until you read what comes next!   In the previous chapter we saw the spectacle of a house wracked by tension and dissension, with the mother as the source.

Next, we consider another household that experiences great trouble in large part because of the *husband*.   We met this man in the previous chapter.   As a matter of fact, he was in the running to be the villain of the piece.

That person is Jacob.   A man whose very name means grasper or deceiver, he lives up--or should we say down--to that name.   And yet, in God's sovereign grace, Jacob is elected to be formed more and more into God's image, until we meet him blessing his grandchildren at the end of his life.

"With believers it may rain in the morning, thunder at midday, and pour torrents in the afternoon, but it must clear up before the sun goes down."   This is very true of Jacob.

To paraphrase one writer: Jacob had a stormy passage, but the waters were smooth as he entered the port.

Many of his hours were cloudy and dark, "but the sunset bathed it with radiant splendor at its close."

Before basking in the golden rays of Jacob's sunset, we need to be aware of some of the storms that occurred between his tricking the blessing out of his father Isaac and until he himself blesses people and worships God with his last breaths.

81

First, let's look at **Jacob's Journey: From Exile to Egypt**. In this chapter we will look at Jacob's life from his exile due to fear of Esau to his sojourn in Egypt. When last we saw Jacob, he had left his father's presence, and his brother Esau had discovered he had been tricked out of his blessing.

We read that Esau holds a grudge against Jacob because of that. Esau says to himself, "'The days of mourning for my father are near; then I will kill my brother Jacob.'"

As usual, Rebekah hears about it. She decides that sending Jacob away is better than allowing Esau to kill him. So she sends him to her brother Laban, who lives in what today would be northern Syria or western Iraq.

On the way, Jacob has what is one of the most significant spiritual encounters of his life. While sleeping one night he has a dream. He sees a ladder going from earth to heaven with God's angels going up and down it.

At the top of the ladder or stairway, the Lord speaks to Jacob, "'I am the LORD, the God of your father Abraham and the God of Isaac.... All people on earth will be blessed through you and your offspring. I am with you and will watch over you wherever you go, and I will bring you back to this land. I will not leave you until I have done what I have promised you.'"

Jacob wakes up and says, "'Wow! Surely the LORD is in this place.'" He is rightly afraid and says, "'How awesome is this place! This is none other than the house of God; this is the gate of heaven.'"

So Jacob names the place Bethel, which means the house of God. He builds a pillar to remind himself of this encounter. He also makes a vow and promises to give God a tenth of everything God gives him.

Eventually Jacob arrives in Paddan Aram and there he meets his match in trickery--his uncle Laban. He learns that deceitfulness runs in the family. First Laban pulls the old bait and switch by giving Jacob Leah as his wife under the cover of darkness. Altogether, Jacob put in 14 years of work for his two wives. And the troubles were just beginning.

The two wives begin to have a baby race. Leah eventually has eleven children and Rachel has two--Joseph in Paddan and Benjamin later.

Laban next tries to steal Jacob's wealth. That is thwarted. Eventually Laban gets outraged at being outsmarted.

So Jacob flees again--this time with two wives, eleven sons, one daughter and a bunch of livestock.

As Jacob returns home he gets scared about meeting Esau. The night before that meeting, he has another very significant experience with God. He struggles over this with God.

Esau and Jacob are reconciled, but the children are growing up and they start getting into more complications than the Ewing family on that old night time soap opera called "Dallas."

Jacob experiences the double blow of the death of his father and then the death of his beloved wife, Rachel, as she gives birth to Benjamin.

What follows is perhaps even more distressing. Joseph reports a dream that upsets his brothers because it indicates they will one day bow down to him.

They respond inappropriately by selling Joseph into slavery and faking his death. Jacob's grief is bitter.

You might know the rest of the story. Maybe you have seen the musical "Joseph and the Amazing Technicolor Coat." Joseph is taken to Egypt, is wrongfully imprisoned, eventually becomes pharaoh's right hand man, and saves the Middle East from the worst of a devastating famine.

That famine brings Joseph's half-brothers to Egypt. Joseph

demands that Benjamin be brought to him, which causes further heartache to Jacob.

So Jacob has been through an incredible amount of what today are called life stress units--two moves under stress, marital difficulties, in-law problems, the death of father, wife, and apparently a son, with another put at risk by being sent to Egypt.

But joy does dawn for Jacob. He comes to Egypt where his son is the second most powerful person in the land.

But the pomp of Egypt does not turn Jacob's head. When he is in the presence of Pharaoh, it is *Jacob* who blesses Pharaoh-- and the rule is that the greater blesses the lesser. He wants to bless his children with the faith of the true God. He wants to be buried in the Promised Land.

Jacob is preparing to die by faith. "To die by faith, we must... live by faith. And a life of faith is not like the shining of the sun on a calm and clear day, its rays meeting with no resistance from the atmosphere; rather [it is] more like the sun rising on a foggy morning, its rays struggling to pierce through and dispel the opposing mist."

"It [is] during the closing days of his life that Jacob's faith [shines] most brightly."

It shines when he gives permission for Benjamin to go to Egypt. It glows before Pharaoh. "With becoming dignity he conducts himself as a child of the King of Kings... and carries himself as becomes an ambassador of the most high."

But Jacob's faith is best seen when he blesses his children and worships God.

In Genesis 49, he blesses his sons by Leah, most notably the line of Judah that would one day have a ruler who will receive the obedience of all nations--that person being none other than Jesus Christ.

But the writer of the Book of Hebrews, when he considers

the faith of Jacob, lifts up the chapter before the 49th of Genesis when he writes, "By faith Jacob, when he was dying blessed each of Joseph's sons, and worshiped as he leaned on top of his staff."

When we come to the Jacob niche in the second Genesis Corridor of the Hall of Faith, we behold him blessing Joseph's sons and worshiping God.

Jacob blesses Joseph's sons in Genesis 48. In verses 1 through 14 Jacob reviews God's dealings. He speaks of God Almighty, El Shaddai who appeared to him at Bethel. He speaks of Joseph's sons---Ephraim and Mannaseh--and prepares to bless the younger over the older.

Verses 15&16 contain the actual blessing, while verses 17-19 give a sense of *deja vu*, as the son--in this case Joseph--tries to get the father--Jacob who also named Israel by God--to bless the elder grandson first.

Verse 20 contains further blessing. This chapter contains numerous parallels with the previous chapter. The blesser is old. He blesses the younger over the older. He blesses both of them "concerning things to come, as he himself had been blessed by Isaac." Jacob shows a faith similar to that of Isaac.

There is a major difference, however, between the two blessers. Isaac was misled by the plotting of his wife and younger son regarding the blessing [that] he had designed for the elder; but when Jacob on his deathbed blessed the two sons of Joseph he *deliberately* bestowed the greater blessing on Ephraim, the younger son."

"While Jacob's earlier career had been marked by anything but faith, as he tried repeatedly by his own scheming to gain advantage for himself, yet at the end of his days he recognized the futility of all his scheming, and relied on the faithfulness of the 'Mighty One of Israel.'"

Jacob blessed. **Jacob worshiped.** For that, we need to

back up to the end of Genesis 47. It is there, in verse 31, that we see "the picture of the patriarch sitting on his bed and leaning on his staff."

It comes after Joseph assures his father, taking the equivalent of a court room oath, that Jacob will be buried with Isaac and Abraham.

It would be something like my having my remains returned to Riverside, California. Or like a Floyd County, Iowa, native would die out of state having previously requested to be put to rest in a cemetery in Charles City, Iowa. In Jacob's case "it was far more than a sentimental whim which moved the patriarch to desire that his body be buried in the Holy Land: it was the working of faith, a blessed exhibition of his confidence in God."

"Having secured the promise from Joseph that his will should be carried out, Jacob bowed before God in worship, for now he realized the LORD was making good the promise recorded in Genesis 46: where God says, 'I will go down to Egypt with you, and I will surely bring you back again. And Joseph's own hand will close your eyes.'"

Jacob's act of worship signifies "his complete dependence upon God, testifies to his condition as a pilgrim [on] the earth, and emphasizes his weariness of the world and his readiness to part from it."

It is blessed "to find that that Holy Spirit's final word about Jacob in Scripture... depicts him in the act of worship."

What can we learn from the life and death of Jacob? We learn about **people** and our need to be sensitive to those going through the wringer. Listen and do not be quick to judge. Encourage them to follow in the way of the LORD.

We learn about **ourselves**. Let us consider how we may be too much like Jacob in his earlier years--stubborn, selfish and shameful.

We learn about **faith**. God gave Jacob a new name--Israel--which means "he who strives with God." Instead of grasping on his own, Jacob learns to strive with God in prayer.

That is good. Jesus calls us to persevere in prayer. We read of Paul working at prayer, striving with God in the sense of laying hold of the promises.

May we have the faith of Israel as we bless others and worship **God**, about Whom we also learn. He is faithful, isn't he? Jacob messes up over and over again, while God remains true. Jacob is consistent in his inconsistency, while God is faithful.

"I will bless you," says God, but most of all, "*I* will be with you."

When it comes to the Lord's Supper, we are so grateful for God giving us the ultimate blessing of forgiveness of sin through the death of His Son.

Jesus is with us during the partaking of the elements--His real spiritual presence is brought to us by His Holy Spirit.

And, for those who follow Him and worship Him in spirit and in truth and follow His commandments, He assures us of His enduring presence, "'Behold, I am with you always--even to the end of the age.'"

- Section 13 -

Joseph

By an act of faith, Joseph, while dying, prophesied the exodus of Israel, and made arrangements for his own burial.

Hebrews 11:22   The Message

I have preached the material in this chapter on Memorial Day Sunday. I have been at many grave side services when veterans are honored. The flag is folded and given to the closest survivor. Sometimes flags are flown at half-mast after the death of someone--a soldier, president, or someone else.

When it comes to finishing well, living out the Christian faith at the end our life, "God is greatly glorified when His people leave this world with their flag flying at full mast."

"When the spirit triumphs over the flesh, when the world is consciously and gladly left behind for heaven."

Such is the case with Joseph, son of Jacob. In his final moments, we behold an unflagging faith, a faith flying at full mast.

Joseph prepares for death. But he has also experienced various kinds of death throughout his life. Let's look first at the

Deaths in the life of Joseph. We have heard of dying a thousand deaths. Each one of us knows what it is like to have things that feel like death in various areas.

Some of us have known betrayal. I am sure that all of us have experienced disappointment in various ways. We have been denied jobs or other things. We have felt the death of a thousand cuts of pettiness. And there is the awful feeling of death through separation.

Did you know that Joseph experiences each one of those "deaths"? Let's look at two specific kinds of death in the life of Joseph. First there is enslavement. At the age of seventeen,

Joseph's brothers sell him into slavery. How did this horrible event happen?

It began when Joseph started telling his brothers about dreams he was having. The clear meaning of the dreams was that someday all of his brothers would bow down to him.

As you can imagine, that did not sit well with the brothers! So, they eventually lured him into the country and put him into a hole. They were going to kill him outright, but one of his brothers convinces the rest to sell him into slavery instead.

Jacob is presented with fabricated evidence that makes it look like Joseph was killed by a wild animal. As far as he knows, Joseph is dead, and he grieves accordingly.

Joseph goes to Egypt and is sold to Potiphar, who is a high ranking official. God blesses Joseph so much that Potiphar completely trusts him to take care of all his business.

But then Potiphar's wife tries to seduce Joseph. When he says no, the wife screams out and accuses him of having accosted her. That is when Joseph experiences another sort of death-- wrongful imprisonment.

He is put in jail for doing the right thing. That must have doubled the feeling of "death" in jail. But, once again God blesses Joseph. The head jailer basically puts Joseph in charge of the prison.

A couple other prisoners have dreams and Joseph interprets them. Eventually one of the released prisoners tells Pharaoh about Joseph.

Joseph interprets Pharaoh's dreams to mean seven years of bumper crops, followed by seven years of devastating lack of crops.

Pharaoh elevates Joseph to be his right hand man and to take care of preparing for the famine. The famine eventually forces Joseph's brothers to travel to Egypt seeking food.

Not knowing that he is their brother, his brothers bow down before him. The dream is fulfilled, but not after Joseph has experienced major deaths of enslavement and imprisonment.

We can learn from the cycles of Joseph's life. The late Ray Ortlund talked about the "A," "B," and "C" zones.

There is the "A" zone where Joseph has the vision or dream of what is going to happen. That is very exciting. We have all had such experiences.

But then we hit the "B" zone. Things happen that are unpleasant. We do not want to keep going because there is pain and hurt. Sometimes pastors do this--they take another church rather than work with people with God's help in working through the challenges.

So they (and we!) try to return to the A zone. If we keep doing that then we miss out on the "C" zone. The C zone is where we see the fulfillment of what we saw in the A zone. But it is much deeper and richer because of having gone through the B zone.

Joseph goes through the B zone. God brings him to the C zone. Not only do his brothers bow before him, but they eventually join him in Egypt and he is reunited with his father Jacob who is re-named Israel.

Israel sees Joseph's two sons. Joseph lives out the rest of his life with joy. And that leads us to

Faith at the death of Joseph. As we consider physical death, it would be helpful to realize that instead of fearing death as the Grim Reaper, those who belong to Christ may welcome it as the International Harvester!

Joseph gives a prophecy about the Exodus, about which we read in Genesis 50:24. Here is how *The Message* Bible puts it: "At the end, Joseph said to his brothers, 'I am ready to die. God will most certainly pay you a visit and take you out of this land and back to the land he so solemnly promised to Abraham, Isaac, and

Jacob.'"

We read of Joseph's certain faith in how we can rely on God. Joseph says, "God *surely* will do this."

"Joseph, at the very time of his death, was engaged with the future happiness of God's people. True faith not only desires that it shall be well with our own soul, but with the church at large."

And what is it that God will do? God will visit his people. This looks forward to the Israelites' Exodus from Egypt. God visits and rescues his people from the imprisonment of slavery.

"Ignorance may exclude terror... but there can be no true peace, no firm confidence, no triumphant joy for those" who are not in Christ. "Only someone who possesses genuine faith can die worshipping and glorifying God for his promises."

With that we move to Joseph's provision for burial, as found in Genesis 50:25-- "Then Joseph made the sons of Israel promise under oath, 'When God makes his visitation, make sure you take my bones with you as you leave here.'"

To Joseph "Egypt was nothing in comparison with Canaan." "Neither the riches nor the honor of Egypt could secure Joseph from death, nor did they make him unmindful or afraid of it.

"Faith is gifted with long-distant sight, and therefore it is able to look beyond all the hills and mountains of difficulty into the shining horizons of the divine promises."

Here are the reasons for Joseph making this request. He wants to show his belief in the promises of the LORD. He confirms the future saga of God's people. And, he wants to "establish a public memorial, by which on all occasions his posterity might call to mind the truth of the promise."

My grandfather Corr retired from practicing medicine when he was 75. When people would bug him about why he had retired he would say, "I am putting things in a dying condition!"

That would pretty much end the conversation. And, by God's grace, he lived another 22 years--almost all of which were spent in active living.

He also would quote Shakespeare--much to the displeasure of my step-grandmother. Shakespeare wrote about "shuffling off this mortal coil."

With Joseph we see at the end of his life putting things in a dying condition. He was prepared to shuffle off the mortal coil. As I have observed some elderly people as they near death, I have seen that God helps them in making the transition and preparing them for eternal life with Him--the five senses wane and their sense for God grows.

Which brings us to Yusuf, which is another way of saying Joseph. Do you notice how the Book of Genesis ends? In chapter 50 verse 26, we read that "Joseph died at the age of 110 years. They embalmed him and placed him in a coffin in Egypt."

Did you catch that? He is embalmed and put in a coffin. But there is no mention of a burial.

Keil and Delitzsch write that Joseph "was placed in an ordinary coffin constructed of sycamore wood. The coffin was then put in a room, according to Egyptian custom and stayed in Egypt for 360 years, 'until [the Israelites] carried it away with them at the time of the Exodus, when it was eventually buried in Shechem, in the piece of land which had been bought by Jacob there." We read about the burial in Joshua 24:32.

"Thus the account of the Pilgrims--[the] life of the Patriarchs [ends] with an act of faith on the part of the dying Joseph; and after his death, [as a result of] his instructions, the coffin with his bones became a standing exhortation to Israel, to turn its eyes away from Egypt to Canaan, the land promised to its fathers, and to wait in the patience of faith for the fulfillment of the promise."

As we wrap up our tour through the second Genesis

corridor, it is important for people of any age to prepare for death. I am not talking about being morbid. We are to enjoy life to the fullest in all seasons of life.

Regardless of our circumstances we can know the joy of the Lord. And, God has put us together to want to be alive on earth for many decades. But it is helpful to keep short accounts with each other, to reconcile whenever possible. And, it is also a loving thing to prepare a will or trust, as well as have medical and financial powers of attorney in place before they are needed.

But most important is to make sure that each one of us has a right relationship with God. Are we walking with Jesus each day? Digging into His written Word? Communicating with Him through prayer? Participating in a small group Bible study? Regularly attending a public service where God is worshiped in spirit and in truth?

As we do that, God will lift our eyes to seek the blessing of others--in the church, our community and around the world.

James M. Boice quotes Charles H Spurgeon on this subject in his commentary on the Gospel of John: "As long as there is breath in our bodies, let us serve Christ; as long as we can think, as long as we can speak, as long as we can work, let us serve Him, let us serve Him with our last gasp, and, if it be possible, let us try to set some work going that will glorify Him when we are dead and gone."

Joseph experienced various kinds of death in his life. Yet God made him a blessing to others and caused him to grow through those experiences. Then, when the end came here on earth, he finished well. It was well with Joseph's soul. Is it well with yours?

"When peace, like a river, attendeth my way,

When sorrows like sea billows roll;

Whatever my lot, Thou has taught me to say,

It is well, it is well, with my soul."

MOSES WING

- Section 14 -

"Faith at Birth"

By an act of faith, Moses' parents hid him away for three months after his birth. They saw the child's beauty [that he was no ordinary child--NIV], and they braved the king's decree.
Hebrews 11:23 The Message

Do you like babies? I do! They are so cute, cuddly and sweet. But there was a time in Bible history when a national leader did *not* like a certain kind of baby--specifically male Hebrew babies.

In this chapter we enter the Moses Wing. Moses is perhaps better known in our day because of such movies as "The Ten Commandments" and, more recently, "The Prince of Egypt."

But before we look at the faith of Moses, we need to first consider

The faith of his parents. Their names are Amram and Jochebed. We read that they are both of the tribe of Levi. This will be significant later in Moses' life because that group will become the priests of the Old Testament, with Moses' brother Aaron becoming the head of the priests.

Because of the situation in Egypt at the time of his birth, the parents of Moses engage in civil disobedience. It had been many years since Joseph had helped Pharaoh, Egypt, and much of the Middle East in response to a famine. We read in Exodus 1 that "a Pharaoh arose who knew not Joseph."

It gets to the point where Pharaoh commands that all Jewish baby boys be killed upon birth. Were the parents "reckless and foolish? No, indeed, they took their orders from a far higher authority than any earthily potentate."

97

There had already been civil disobedience by mid-wives. We read in the Message Bible that "the midwives had far too much respect for God and didn't do what the king of Egypt ordered; they let the boy babies live."

When the king challenged the midwives about this, they used a dodge, "'The Hebrew women aren't like the Egyptian women; they're vigorous. Before the midwife can get there, they've already had the baby.'"

God honors the midwives for honoring Him in the area of life. We read that "God was pleased with the midwives. Because the midwives honored God, God gave them families of their own."

And this leads to the issue of when civil disobedience is appropriate. Paul teaches in Romans 13 that "everyone must submit himself to the governing authorities, for there is no authority except that which God has established."

"It is true that the LORD requires His people to 'be in subjection to the higher powers,' but this holds good only so long as the... human [ruler] require[s] the Christian to do nothing which God has forbidden *or* prohibit nothing [that] God has commanded."

Civil disobedience is rarely appropriate, but when a human command contradicts a major command of God--especially in the area of life--then a believer must obey God.

A well-known example of God-honoring civil disobedience has to do with Corrie ten Boom and her family. I have written of their being put in a Nazi prison camp. But I have not dwelt on the reason why they were arrested.

For some time, the ten Booms harbored Jews in their home. They hid them in various places and they had a drill to hide the Jews when an unknown visitor came to the door.

The ten Booms lied like the midwives to save lives. But ultimately they were found out and were arrested under a law that contradicted God's law. And every ten Boom but Corrie died because of their efforts to save lives.

In the case of the midwives and the parents of Moses, they did not lose their lives. Had they been discovered they could have been killed; they did engage in civil disobedience.

The parents of Moses saw he was an extraordinary child. Every parent and grandparent rightly claims that their children are special. But there does seem to have been a special anointing by God upon the baby Moses. His extraordinary nature--recognized at an early age--was a "token of divine approval, and a sign that God [had] some special design concerning him."

That leads his parents to hide him for three months. They do this because they are fearful of God, not people. And this is where we see their faith. They fear the God they cannot see instead of the human ruler they very much *can* see. And fear of God here ties in with the faith definition of Hebrews 11:1--"Faith is the assurance of things hoped for, the conviction of things not seen."

"The fear of the LORD was upon them, and therefore they were delivered from that fear of man which brings a snare."

"Their faith is shown in their not obeying the king's commandment, but fulfilling without fear of people all that is required of parental love, which God approves, and which is made all the stronger by the beauty of the child, and in their confident assurance, in spite of all apparent impossibilities, that their effort would be successful."

The midwives and the parents of Moses have an Audience of One--God. They fear only God. This fear is a reverential awe that leads to action, not paralysis.

It is this God Whose sovereignty is seen in the birth and aftermath of the birth of Moses. So we come to the

Sovereignty of God. He sovereignty works everything together

99

for good for those who love Him. Here is how Paul puts it in Romans 8:28, "We know that in all things God works for the good of those who love Him who have been called according to His purpose."

While Pharaoh is urging forward the extermination of the Israelites, God is preparing their emancipation. According to the divine purpose, the murderous edict of the king will "lead to the training and the preparation of the human deliverer of Israel."

God's sovereignty is first seen in the fact of Moses' Levite parents. As mentioned earlier, the priests of the Jewish faith would come from the tribe of Levi--who was one of the sons of Jacob.

The parents of Moses are like the parents of John the Baptist and the parents of Jesus in that they had a faith in God that involved both fear and love.

God's sovereignty is also seen by his parents' placement on the Nile of their son. This is not abandonment. Moses' mother puts Moses into a basket that the Bible calls an "ark." This is meant to remind us of Noah and his ark, through which God brought physical salvation of humans and animal.

As far as the basket ingredients go, bitumen is asphalt to fasten the papyrus stalks. The pitch is to make it water tight. Moses is placed in God's care on the Nile.

God's sovereignty is seen in what happens with Pharaoh's daughter. She comes at the right time to see the basket. She is fully aware that this is a Hebrew child. She is fully aware of her father's decree.

Nevertheless she takes the baby out of the basket and gives the child a name.

And it does not stop there. It turns out that Moses' older sister Miriam has followed along the side of the Nile to see what happens to her brother in the basket.

When Pharaoh's daughter takes Moses out of the water, Miriam comes up to her. Pharaoh's daughter listens to Miriam. She listens to her suggestions. Miriam speaks up. She puts her trust in God to provide speech and to protect her from the possible wrath of Egyptian royalty.

Things work out for Pharaoh's daughter to agree to have Moses' mother raise her son. On top of that, she pays the mother to be the mother! See how God works everything together for good? The mother gets paid. She receives a royal subsidy!

We see here multiple examples of God's sense of humor: the daughter of the one who has commanded the death of Hebrew baby boys--this daughter saves the one whom God will use to save, to deliver the Hebrews. This Hebrew child--born of Levite parents--will be raised as a prince.

The daughter of Pharaoh adopts Moses. She educates him. He receives the best education that the high Egyptian culture can offer. It is a combination of a Harvard MBA and Public Policy Ph.D. He receives "thoroughly Egyptian training, and [is] educated in all the wisdom of the Egyptians," as Stephen states in Acts 7:22" as he gives a brief history of the Israelites.

"Through such an education..., [Moses] receives just the training required for the performance of the work to which God [would] call him. Thus the wisdom of Egypt is employed by the wisdom of God for the establishment of the Kingdom of God."

God prepares him to be the deliverer. This is seen in the name of Moses. At the time of Jesus we read that "the Egyptians call water *Mo* and those who are rescued from the water *uses*."

To us, it refers "to the importance of the person rescued from the water to the Israelite nation."

Whether it is the faith of Moses' parents or all the ways God sovereignly works in the life of Moses, this all fits into God's bigger plan. God can overrule any situation.

Does the head of a nation decree the death of all Hebrew boys? God works it out to have a Hebrew boy adopted by that ruler's daughter!

Not only that, she pays his mother to raise him. She sees that he receives education and training that will help prepare him to lead God's people out of bondage and to the threshold of the Promised Land.

Maybe you are having problems sorting out what is going on in your life or in the world. There all kinds of circumstances and events swirling around that could be confusing you or maybe even depressing you.

I would encourage you to dig into God's written Word and learn God's clearly revealed will for your life. As you take practical steps--guided by God's Holy Spirit--to live for Him, then you will begin to see and understand God's larger plan for your life and beyond.

In *That Hideous Strength*, C. S. Lewis writes about "the great dance." He writes of each person's life being a dance. And how that dance interacts with others and how those dances are part of ever larger and more intricate dances.

The dance theme shows how God works everything together for good. As we understand and rejoice in this reality we find our love for God growing ever stronger.

- Section 15 -

"Royal Son—Man's Way or God's Way?"

By faith, Moses, when grown, refused the privileges of the Egyptian
royal house.
Hebrews 11:24   The Message

As a young man, he knew what his life's work would be.
His ambition was to write *the* book about the "Glorious Revolution"
of the Bolsheviks.

He would write that book alright, but not in the way he
imagined.   He would come to write a series of historical novels
about those years that shook the world, but he would do so only
after the following things happened:

*he was deprived of his freedom for fifteen years because of a letter
he wrote to a friend.   In that letter this World War Two artillery
gunner included a sarcastic reference to Stalin.

*He would get cancer.

*He would eventually be kicked out of his beloved country and
come to live in Vermont.

The name of the man is Alexander Isayavich Solzhenitsyn.
He fulfilled his life's ambition alright, but with a radically different
conclusion.   His books on the revolution showed that it was not
glorious.   He learned that sometimes man's way is not God's way.

There once was another young man who understood what
his life's work was to be.   He was very zealous to be about that
work as he approached his 40th birthday.   But he needed to
understand that God's timetable is often quite different from ours.
The name of this man is Moses.   As we consider this royal son from
the perspectives of Hebrews 11:24 and then Exodus 2:11-15, I hope
we will ask ourselves this question, "Which is better--man's way or

God's way?"

In **Hebrews 11:24** we learn that Moses has been raised as an Egyptian Prince, yet by faith he refuses to be known as the son of Pharaoh's daughter. The word "refuse" means to "disdain."

Moses takes a stand of faith. He renounces the status that he enjoys "in Egypt as a member of the royal household. He cannot identify himself both with the Israelites and with the Egyptians; he has to choose one or the other."

He chooses God's way, and in so doing **He gives up some things**, including royal privilege and power. We need to remember what possibilities Moses has. He is "one of those in whom genius and opportunity have met together."

He has been trained in all the wisdom of the Egyptians, and there is no sphere short of the throne itself that he could not fill, and fill in a worthy manner.

In Egypt, during Moses' time, there seems to be everything that could satisfy the loftiest aspirations. Egypt is a great empire. She vies with Babylon as a center of art and science, and as a home of culture.

If Moses chooses for Egypt, here are his options--depending on his preferences:

*In the realm of war, "he might have won fame as a great leader and strategist."

*In the area of diplomacy "he could hold his own with the best statesmen of foreign countries."

If he stays in the palace he could become "a second Joseph, the virtual ruler of the land."

The writer of the Book of Hebrews "presents Moses to us at the parting of the ways. Moses resolutely refuses to walk along the alluring Egyptian path. He gives up much."

What does Moses gain? For starters, try uncertainty,

poverty and hard work.

But he also knows the joy of obedience, of obeying God and trusting in Him. I am reminded of Paul the Apostle, who writes to his Philippian friends: "If anyone else thinks he has reasons to put confidence in the flesh, I have more: circumcised on the eighth day, of the people of Israel, of the tribe of Benjamin, a Hebrew of Hebrews; in regard to the law, a Pharisee; as for zeal, persecuting the church; as far as legalistic righteousness, faultless.

"But whatever was to my profit I now consider loss for the sake of Christ. What is more, I consider everything a loss compared to the surpassing greatness of knowing Christ Jesus my Lord, for whose sake I have lost all things. I consider them rubbish, that I may gain Christ and be found in Him, not having a righteousness of my own that comes from the law, but that which is through faith in Christ--the righteousness that comes from God and is by faith. I want to know Christ and the power of His resurrection and the fellowship of sharing in his sufferings, becoming like Him in His death, and so, somehow, to attain to the resurrection of the dead."

Paul chooses God's way--the way of the cross followed by resurrection. Paul takes the name of Christ, he identifies himself as a Christian, with all the sacrifice and joy that that means.

How about you? Are you willing to walk the Christian way, even if it means ridicule and loss?

Moses identifies himself as belonging to the God of Israel, *not* with the Egyptians and their gods. Moses has to ask himself the question, "To whom do I belong? The house of Pharaoh or the House of God?"

And we need to ask ourselves, "Are we putting anyone or anything ahead of God in our affections?"

There is a temptation here. Moses might have thought, or someone might have suggested to him, "Stay in the house of

Pharaoh. Why sacrifice a fulcrum that gives you such leverage and try to raise your people by a dead lift?"

But that is man's way, not God's way. That Moses chooses for God is clear in Hebrews 3:2-- "Moses was faithful in all God's house."

To see Moses' first steps along God's way, we turn to **Exodus 2:11-25**, where we meet a person who has a lot to learn. Moses has grown up physically; he has even chosen the right path. But it is time to start growing up spiritually.

He sees the burden of his people, how they are oppressed by the very Pharaoh in whose house he lives. Moses goes and sees. He is faced with the dilemma of bringing about deliverance in man's way or God's way. He chooses the most direct method, which turns out to be the wrong one.

He kills an Egyptian he sees beating a Hebrew person. He thinks that the end justifies the means. That is something we need to guard against in our own lives.

Moses does it his way, using man's ways:

*He checks to make sure no one sees him.

*He literally takes matters into his own hands and kills the Egyptian.

*He then tries to conceal, to cover up, the evidence by hiding the dead man in the sand.

God's way is not concerned with whether one will be caught. At a later time, God will strike the Egyptian nation because of Pharaoh's hard heart. God does not conceal, rather he reveals.

The comparison between man's way--which Moses takes in trying to help--and God's way in God's time, points up the bankruptcy of what is known as **Liberation Theology**.

Liberation Theology claims that man is the master of his

own destiny. It is a political theology that has joined hands with Marxism, which should be an indication to you where God fits in-- because Marxism is atheistic at its core, God does not fit in with this system.

Liberation Theology is a horizontal theology, which basically has man liberating man from economic and political oppression.

Those who hold to Liberation Theology can sometimes be rather oppressive themselves. I know of a student at a seminary some years ago who suffered at the hands of a professor because the student dared to write a paper that challenged some points of Liberation Theology.

Furthermore, Liberation Theology offers no true hope for deliverance from that which binds so horribly--over sin against separation from God. As Paul writes, "If only for this life we have hope in Christ, we are to be pitied more than all men."

That which truly liberates is the truth of God in Christ. It is God who liberates totally and completely--in His way and in His time. Do you believe this?

That is what Moses needs to learn before he can be used by God to bring liberation to the people of Israel.

For a training ground, Moses is sent into the wilderness. He flees after he discovers that the murder is no longer a secret. That news is found in the words of a fellow Hebrew. The day after the murder, Moses sees two Hebrews fighting. Moses asks the one who has picked the fight, "Why are you hitting your fellow Hebrew?"

The man replies, "Who made you ruler and judge over us? Are you thinking of killing me as you killed the Egyptian?"

Moses realizes that the jig is up. He sees that man's way brings about messy consequences. He has two choices:

*stay and face the music; or

*leave to do battle another day in God's way.

He goes to the southern part of the Sinai Peninsula where he marries Zipporah and has a son whom he names Gershom. Gershom means "an alien there."

I am reminded again of Alexander Solzhenitsyn. He was imprisoned for ten years, and then experienced internal exile for another five. He was banished to Kazakhstan.

And then--until the Fall of the Soviet Union--he was banished from his home country and was an alien in the United States. Many did not know how to respond to him. Many still probably do not have him figured out.

Doubtless, many were not sure how to deal with Moses-- this man who carries himself like a Pharaoh and gives every outward sign of being an Egyptian--yet he has identified with the oppressed Hebrews.

But God is preparing Moses to deliver his people in God's way and in God's time.

We read at the end of Exodus two, "God heard their groaning and he remembered His covenant with Abraham, with Isaac and with Jacob. So God looked on the Israelites and was concerned about them."

And God is concerned about and for you. Whatever you are going through. He is concerned that you not be led astray by people, beliefs, or a lifestyle that stops at a dead end.

He is concerned enough to want you to know that saving faith begins with and includes "a deliberate renunciation or turning away from all that is opposed to God, a determination to utterly deny self and [to choose] to submit to whatever trials may be byproducts of a life of" faith.

Being a Christian means to ask questions and to know the answers. It means asking, "Is this man's way or God's way?"

Being a Christian means being open to the guidance of the Holy Spirit, even if that means you will not be as comfortable as you would like to be.

It means being careful to not try to save yourself on your own. We all have our subtle ways of trying to work or earn our way to heaven. Remember that all the other religions in the world tell people to work their way to heaven, which is not possible to do.

Both of these--comfort and self-salvation--must be renounced and crucified. The life of ease must be submitted to Christ. Self-salvation must be given up as hopeless, with your hope put fully in Jesus and His saving power.

It comes down to a question of choice. Will you choose the way of the world that will pass to dust? Or will you choose the way of God who endures forever, as does His written word and as do His people. I encourage you to choose God's way.

Let God lift you to Himself as you choose to follow in *His* way. Christianity is the only faith that is a *relationship* not a religion. In Christ, God has reached down in love and lifted us to Himself.

"All my heart to Him I give, ever to Him I'll cling

In His blessed presence live, ever His praises sing,

Love so mighty and so true, merits my soul's best songs,

Faithful, loving service too, to Him belongs.

"Love lifted me! Love lifted me!

When nothing else could help

Love lifted me!"

- Section 16 -

"Excuses, Excuses, Excuses"

Moses "said, "Oh, [LORD], please! Send somebody else!'
"God got angry with Moses: 'Don't you have a brother, Aaron the
Levite? He's good with words, I know he is.... I'll be right there with
you as you speak and with him as he speaks, teaching you step by
step.'"
Exodus 4

Have you ever made an excuse?   Do you know of someone else who has?   There are different kinds of excuses, but we usually recognize them for what they are--poor excuses, lame excuses.

Did you know that during one part of his life, the great leader Moses was as good as anyone at giving excuses?   That's right: one of the two men who qualifies for his own wing in the Hall of Faith had challenges and experienced failures just like we do.

This particular instance is reported to us in Exodus 3-4:17. I invite you to open your Bible and read along (out loud for best effect?) in each section.

The verses of Exodus 3:1-10 **set the stage** for Moses giving excuse after excuse.   Of everything read in this chapter, this passage is probably the most familiar to you.   It has to do with Moses and God at the burning bush.   There are many lessons, including how holy God is and how we are to respond to Him.

It tells us of God's concern for His people and of the promise He makes to bring the Israelites out of Egypt.

The rub comes in verse ten.   The reason why Moses comes up with at least four excuses is because God says to Moses, "I am sending **you** to Pharaoh to bring my people the Israelites out of Egypt."

111

Read verses eleven and twelve of Exodus chapter three for **Moses' first excuse and God's response.** Moses asks God, "Who am I?" To a certain extent, Moses questions his own identity. Even more than that, he has learned to not trust himself.

"Moses, unlike his early days in Egypt, has learned to distrust himself so thoroughly that he will incur God's anger [in verse 14 of the next chapter]. Self-distrust is good, but only when it leads to trust in God. Otherwise it ends as spiritual paralysis-- the inability and unwillingness to undertake any course of action."

Moses expresses his disbelief that God could use him. It is as if Moses is saying to God, "You've got the wrong guy. We're talking damaged goods here."

Because God loves Moses and because God will not be turned from His purpose, He does not let Moses get away with this or any other excuse.

God's response to Moses' excuse #1--who am I?--is a two-fold promise: "I will be with you and I will give you a sign for proof. God's response is one of presence and provision. I will be with you, I will be present. You do not need to worry."

Also, God says "I will give you a sign for proof, but it requires faith in me." That sign, that proof that I have sent you to deliver Israel, is that one day you will return to this mountain and worship God here."

That opens the door to **the second excuse and God's response**. Read Exodus 3:13-21 and you will see that Moses' second excuse has to do with God's identity. Who are you? What's your Name? What shall I tell the people about you? The people may well challenge me with the question, "Under what new title has God appeared to you?"

That means that the people may want to know what new revelation Moses has received from God.

This excuse is responded to by God in verses 14&15. God

says that His name is, "I AM Who I Am." "This is what you are to say to the Israelites: 'I AM has sent me to you.'"

YAHWEH, or Jehovah, is His Name. God is telling Moses, "I will only be understood by my own subsequent acts and words of revelation."

"The revelation of the Name therefore is not merely a deep theological truth; it is a call to the response of faith by Moses and Israel."

God does not stop here in His response to Moses' second excuse. He continues on to give a commandment and promises in verses 15-21. The commandment actually breaks down into three commandments that are of a piece: go, assemble (the elders/the leaders of Israel), and speak to them.

Moses is to tell them God's Name, that God has appeared to Moses and seen what has been done to God's people in Egypt.

The promises are found within what Moses is to say to Israel's leaders: "I have promised to bring you up out of your misery... [and] into a land flowing with milk and honey.

More promises follow, but they revolve around that one of deliverance *from* and deliverance *to*.

This is still not enough for Moses who gives his **third excuse** in Exodus 4:1. The third excuse by Moses shows his insecurity. What if they don't believe me? What if they won't even listen to me? "Moses is still thinking of that bitter experience [recorded in Exodus 2:14] when he was asked, 'Who made you a prince and a judge over us.'"

God responds by giving tangible, visible signs or proofs of Moses' authority. But Moses has one more excuse. Maybe he has been saving this one as his guaranteed out.

Moses' **fourth excuse** is that he is not a good speaker. "What can I do? I am slow of speech and of tongue."

113

Moses may have had a stutter, just as the Apostle Paul might have. If it is possible for God to be characterized as being ticked off, I would say that is a fair assessment of verses 11&12 when God responds with questions. God's had it with Moses. He gives him the command--go, and I will help you speak and will teach you what to say."

But Moses makes one last attempt to wriggle out of his destiny. We see this in Exodus 4:13-17, where **Moses is without excuse.**

Moses is reduced to whining like a child, "Please don't make me do it." It would be so easy for me to point an accusing, self-righteous finger at Moses, except that so often I hear myself thinking--if not saying--"Here I am Lord, send *him*, the other guy."

God responds, first with anger and then with provision. "OK. How about your brother Aaron? He can speak well. I'll tell you what needs to be said and Aaron will be the mouth-piece, the spokesman."

It has been a struggle. Moses has tried as hard as possible to resist God's call. He has given excuse after excuse after excuse after excuse. When God makes him realize that he is without excuse, Moses *does* obey. That is the bottom line. Moses could have saved himself some time and aggravation by saying yes early, but he does finally obey.

With that, we come to **application** of this passage. What can we learn from this true story? There are at least three principles for living.

First: **God's will is not to be run from, but embraced with joy.** Yet, we so often are much like Moses. We seem to be blind to the fact that God wants the best for us. The best means living for His glory, living for Him in every area of my life. The title of a devotional book sums it up well: *My Utmost for His Highest.*

The second lesson is that **God calls and chooses, it is not up**

to us to choose. Moses did not decide he would lead Israel. When God meets Moses at the burning bush, it is clear that leading Israel is the last thing Moses wants to do.

I have learned never to say never to God. Back when I was in High School I had the privilege one weekend of serving tables at a Junior High Camp--what today would be called Middle Schoolers.

As I observed the behavior of some of the Middle Schoolers I thought to myself, I *never* want to work with Junior High students.

I could almost hear God saying, "That's interesting. Guess what I have in mind for you?" Within a year I had been asked to start a Junior High Young Life Group. With God's help I started it from scratch at what had been my Junior High!

The third principle is that **when God calls and chooses, He has equipped us with the tools necessary for the job.**

At the time of lend-lease during the early part of World War Two, Winston Churchill said to the United States, "Give us the tools and we will finish the job!" The most important equipping is the presence of Jesus Christ by the Holy Spirit. With that comes God's power and God's provision. Let's take our eyes off ourselves and look to God. Let's stop giving excuses and start obeying God's good and perfect will.

God revealed Himself to Moses as an all-consuming fire. May we burn with the inner zeal of devotion from the Holy Spirit.

"Teach me to love thee as thine angels love,

One holy passion filling all my frame;

The baptism of the heaven-descended Dove.

My heart an altar, and they love a flame."

- Section 17 -

"Reward of Faith"

Moses valued suffering in the Messiah's camp far greater than Egyptian wealth because he was looking ahead, anticipating the payoff. By an act of faith, he turned his heel on Egypt, indifferent to the king's blind rage.
Hebrews 11:25   The Message

and   "Faith in the Unseen God"

He had his eye on the One no eye can see, and kept right on going. By an act of faith, he kept the Passover Feast and sprinkled Passover blood on each house so that the destroyer of the firstborn wouldn't touch them.
Hebrews 11:27&28

The above verses are found in the midst of the Moses Wing. Hebrews11:25 speaks of "the reward of faith." This leads to verses 26 through 28, which talk faith in the unseen God.   These verses remind us of the second half of the operative definition of faith found in verse one, "Faith is being... certain of what we do not see."

As we consider the faith of Moses, we realize that he had faith in the unseen God who is the God of Passover.

Moses has **faith in the unseen God**.   It is by this kind of faith that Moses leaves Egypt.   The leaving here speaks of the preparation as well as the actual departure.   Moses' faith reminds me of the faith that belonged to Helen Steiner Rice, the famous Christian poet.

She had many challenges in life.   She was able to live normally in plenty and was able to carry on after the death of her husband following the Crash of 1929.

I think of her because of what Moses leaves behind.

117

Whenever he visits the court of Pharaoh to demand that Pharaoh let the people go, Moses is reminded of what he is leaving behind. He is leaving behind the palace, pomp and power of Pharaoh's court.

He sees the opulent rooms, the servants he once had, even his adoptive relatives. But by faith Moses leaves these behind.

With the Apostle Paul he can say, "Whatever was to my profit I now consider loss for the sake of Christ." He has already left Egypt behind in his mind by an act of will, by choosing to stand with God's people.

Now he is preparing to physically leave Egypt. To do so, he is commanded by God to go into the presence of Pharaoh. At the end of Exodus 11, he has done so nine times.

What has Moses received for his efforts? The wrath, the anger of Pharaoh, which can be heard in 11:28, "'Get out of my sight! Make sure you do not appear before me again! The day you see my face you will die.'"

But by faith Moses does not fear Pharaoh's anger. We should not, however, lightly dismiss Pharaoh's anger. His wrath is not to be fooled with. Pharaoh's rage is great. His power to punish at that time was among the greatest in the world. A proverb in the Bible says, "The king's wrath is as the roaring of the lion."

Moses is standing before "a bloody tyrant, armed with all the power of Egypt, threatening him with present death if he persists in the work and duty [that] God has committed to him; but he is so far from being terrified, or declining his duty in the least, that he indicates his resolve to proceed, and announces destruction to the tyrant himself."

Moses fears God instead of Pharaoh. He pays "more attention to the invisible King of kings than to the king of Egypt."

By faith Moses sees the invisible God. He perseveres. He

endures. This is the only time in the Old Testament where this exact word to endure, or persevere, is used. The word "is derived from a root meaning strength or fortitude, to bear evils, undergo dangers with resolution and courage, so as not to faint beneath them, but to hold on our way to the end."

Moses does this because he sees with the eyes of faith. "Moses' lifelong vision of God was the secret of his faith and perseverance."

Moses has faith in the unseen God and **faith in the God of Passover.** This faith involves positive action that keeps negative consequences from occurring.

The positive action by Moses is seen in his ensuring that Passover is kept. "The institution of the Passover was an act of faith, similar to that of Noah's preparation of the ark."

The keeping of Passover also took faith on that first night because the people might have been tempted to flee under cover of darkness. Instead, they stayed inside while the preparations were made and the meal observed.

The second aspect of positive action that Moses takes is in the sprinkling of the blood of the Passover lamb on the threshold of each Israelite home. I will have more to write about that in a little bit.

The positive action taken in faith keeps negative consequences away. "The faith of Moses is displayed in his recognition that God's threat of destruction against the first-born would be accomplished, and that the sprinkling of the blood would ensure the protection of Israel."

A. S. Peake has some interesting information about the sprinkling of blood on door thresholds. "It is a widely spread custom [that] still survives in the [Mid-] East to shed blood on the threshold over which a guest is to pass. He steps over the threshold taking care not to tread upon it, since to trample the blood under foot would mean that he rejected the covenant with insult. There are other suggestions in the Old Testament of the sacredness of the threshold, and there are parallels to it in the history of other peoples. Thus when the Roman bride was taken to her husband's home she was carried across the threshold [so that no slur is cast] on the marriage covenant. If this is so, the thought of the passage is that, while the destroying angel enters into the homes of those who have prepared no welcome for Yahweh, where the blood is sprinkled on the door God passes over the threshold as a welcomed guest, and makes a covenant with [those living] in the house."

You have heard of Moses' faith in the unseen God Who is the God of the Passover. We now come to that part in this chapter where **application** needs to be made. What does this have to do with us? Where does this fit into my life?

I will first look at **the implications of verse 28.** Each one of us needs an active, positive faith. Is your faith operative? Does it play a role in your day to day living?

We need to take God both seriously and joyously. God will have an impact on our lives no matter what we do. It is our decision whether he comes as the bringer of spiritual death or as the welcome landlord.

There are households that make a conscious effort to try to bar entry to the Lord Jesus Christ. Is yours one of them?

Or is it a passive resistance, not giving God a thought until Sunday morning comes or a crisis hits? Don't get me wrong, God can and does reach us through painful experiences. But once the pain passes are you still in relationship with God?

I hope instead that you are learning something of the joy of obedience to the Lord. One of my favorite songs from High School days is called "Free Spirit." It goes something like this,

"Across the gateway of my heart,

I wrote **no thoroughfare**.

120

But love came laughing in,
'I travel anywhere.'
Now I'm a free spirit, happy and free...
Since the Lord has set me free!"

The freedom of that song has to do with the freedom to be obedient to, have **faith and trust in the unseen God**. Do you remember Moses? His faith was in the unseen God. So was Helen Steiner Rice's.

How about yours? Are you more concerned about what has been lost to the past, or what you might be required to leave behind in order to follow Jesus?

"Faith assures the heart of a better portion in return for anything God calls us to relinquish."

By faith, Moses did not fear Pharaoh's anger. "Faith and fear are opposites, and yet... they are often found within the same person; but where one is dominant, the other is dormant." In other words, if faith is dominant in your life, then fear is dormant.

"How the undaunted courage of Moses shows our petty fears!... There are many who fear much less than the wrath of a 'king'--such things as darkness and solitude, or even the rustling of a leaf will frighten them. No doubt such fear is constitutional for some, but with many it is a guilty conscience [that] makes them alarmed at a shadow. The best way for weak ones to overcome their timidity is to be cultivating the sense of God's presence; and for the guilty to confess and forsake their sins."

Proverbs 28:1 says, "The wicked flees when no one is pursuing; but the righteous are bold as a lion." "What was it that enabled Moses to conduct himself with such firmness and boldness? What was it that delivered his heart from fearing the wrath of the king? _Faith_, a spiritual, supernatural, God-given,

God-energized faith." Do you have such faith? May it be so!

May you be like Moses who had faith in the unseen God, who feared only the King of kings. May you and your family make God a welcome guest in your home.

May your life be consecrated to the LORD God, as was Moses and the Israelites!

"Take my life and let it be
Consecrated, Lord, to Thee;
Take my moments and my days,
Let them flow in ceaseless praise.

"Take my will, and make it Thine;
It shall be no longer mine;
Take my heart, it is Thine own;
It shall be Thy royal throne."

- Section 18 -

"Crossing Over in Faith"

"By an act of faith, Israel walked through the Red Sea on dry ground. The Egyptians tried it and drowned."
Hebrews 11:29

In early June of 2008, many communities in Iowa (and a few other states) experienced severe flooding due to two months' worth of rain falling in two days. Some of the members of First Congregational Church of Charles City were directly affected by that weather and river event. It took a while to recover physically and even longer psychologically from all the effects of the flood.

As those dear Iowans came to understand, rivers--and other bodies of water--are very important in the lives of nations and, therefore, also in literature.

I think of the mighty Mississippi into which the Cedar River flows after starting in southern Minnesota and traversing most of the length of Iowa. The Mississippi has played a vital role in the development of the United States. Mark Twain has brought it alive through his writings.

You can go around the world: the Danube in Europe, the Volga in Russia, the Indus in India, and the Amazon in Brazil.

Perhaps one of the most famous rivers--one to which the life of a nation is linked--is the Nile in Egypt.

For the Israelite people, there were two bodies of water that, because of what happened, brought definition to them. The Israelites became a nation after they crossed the Red Sea and went on to receive the law of God at Mount Sinai.

They physically entered the land of their nation when they crossed the Jordan River.

For the Christian, the Red Sea and the Jordan River have come to symbolize two milestones: the beginning and the end of a Christian's life on earth.

Passing through the Red Sea (Paul tells us) is a picture of our baptism. Crossing the River Jordan, as Bunyan's *Pilgrim's Progress* and Negro Spirituals tell us, symbolizes passing from this life to eternal life with God.

In this chapter, our tour of the Hall of Faith brings us to the Red Sea where Moses and the Israelites cross over in faith. They pass through on dry land. But I am getting ahead of myself. In this chapter, I hope to tell the story of the crossing, teach some of what the story means, and apply the story to our lives.

First, I am going to **tell the story** by having you read it section by section and then by having me explain it as needed.

Some background to the story is given in Exodus 13:17-22. There are three sections to this part of the story. First, God makes a mid-course change in the people's itinerary. He does not want the people to immediately face war with the Philistines because the Israelites might want to return to Egypt. So God sends them by the desert road toward the Red Sea.

Next, we learn that Moses is taking the remains of Joseph with him, as prophesied at the end of the book of Genesis. Third, we see that the LORD goes ahead of the people in a pillar of Cloud by day and a pillar of fire by night. As we sing in that great hymn of faith, "Guide me, O Thou Great Jehovah":

"Let the fire and cloudy pillar

Lead me all my journey through."

The prelude to the crossing is found in Exodus 14:1-20. In this passage the LORD speaks to Moses, explaining what He is doing. He is going to draw Pharaoh into pursuit; and pursue Pharaoh does! But when the Israelites see the massive, disciplined Egyptian army led by Pharaoh, the Israelites complain, "What kind of freedom is this? Freedom to die? Slavery in Egypt is preferable to this!"

They have some choice words for Moses. "Didn't we tell you to leave us alone in the first place? This is another fine mess you've gotten us into!"

Moses responds to the people by encouraging them to take their eyes off themselves and the difficulty and to turn to God. "The LORD will fight for you, you need only to be still." Remember the verse in the Psalms where God tells us to "'be still and know that I am God.'"

Then the LORD speaks to Moses. I do not know if it is in response to the prayers or thoughts of Moses, but the LORD reminds Moses of what He will do. He encourages Moses, who sees the angel of God and the pillar deployed to the rear between the Egyptians and the Israelites.

With that, we come to the main event, as told in Exodus 14:21-31. You have probably seen Charleton Heston as Moses portraying this scene. Maybe you have also seen the animated version of the more recent "Prince of Egypt."

Regardless of what you might have seen, you can read in the Bible that: the waters are parted; the people cross over on dry land; the Egyptians pursue; and the waters return and swallow up the Egyptians.

The faith of the Israelites is summed up in verse 31: "And when the Israelites saw the great power the LORD displayed against the Egyptians, the people feared the LORD and put their trust in Him and in Moses His servant."

That story has been told. What is the **teaching** from this passage? Each of the statements, or steps in the background, prelude and the main event have something to teach us.

First, there is the background that shows the guidance of God as he directs the Israelites in the way they are to go. "Guide me, O Thou great Jehovah, pilgrim through this barren land."

The keeping of a promise and the faithfulness of God are evident in the taking of Joseph's remains. Joseph had prophesied the Exodus by saying, "God will surely come to your aid, and then you must carry my bones with you from this place."

The pillars of cloud and fire teach us of the presence of God. He goes before and behind us, as well as within us.

The prelude in Exodus 14:1-20 teaches us many more things.

When the LORD speaks to Moses, we learn that God is the God who communicates and commands.

The pursuit of Pharaoh shows what happens when the pocket book of a wicked person is hit. Pharaoh does not care about keeping the promise he has made.

He could care less about the people who are fleeing. All he knows is that his slave labor is leaving and he would rather fight than lose them.

The prelude also reminds us that the complaining of the Israelites is an all too common, sad pattern. They have done it before with Moses and will do it many more times. In essence, they repeatedly whine, "What have you done for me lately?" It is not only during the time of Moses, but off and on throughout their history.

Moses responds in a pastoral way and the LORD pastors Moses while making Moses aware of his responsibility for being the people's representative before God.

There is much that we learn from the main event. The parting of the waters indicates that nothing is too hard for God. But "why did the sea recede before the Israelites so that they passed over dry-shod? At one level it was an act of God; at another level it could be attributed to the ... wind;" but the writer of Hebrews chooses to focus on "the Israelites' faith. It was nonetheless an act of God, who used the... wind to accomplish His saving purpose, but it was by faith that they 'applied' the deliverance[secured "for them."

The people cross over on dry land because God does things right and because the people have some faith. "There must have been some faith of some kind for them to go forward into the sea at Moses' command."

The pursuit by the Egyptians and the return of the waters show both how God can deal with His enemies and the completeness, thoroughness of God's work, be it in judgment or rescue.

The faith of the Israelites is faith in response to God's action. They have a healthy fear, respectful awe of God. They put their faith in God.

They also put their trust in Moses as God's representative. "The Israelites' faith on this occasion consists in their willingness to go forward at God's word, although it seemed impossible to get across the sea."

From teaching, we move to **applying** some of the lessons to our lives. I will highlight only a few. One is the Israelites' complaining. We are not to whine or be afraid. This is grounded in fear winning out over faith. I mention this for several reasons. One is that I regularly struggle in this area, so I am grateful for God's word to me here.

Maybe you are struggling with fearfulness, a lack of trust in the guidance, presence and provision of God. It is something that each church needs to address. Is your church cowering and complaining, or are we looking to God to see how He will work?

Do you remember how I mentioned in a previous chapter that it is possible for fear and faith to be in the same person? When one is dominant, the other is dormant.

"A faint heart is the worst for a Christian here: when the

anchor of faith is fixed deep in the Rock, he [or she] need never fear the storm; but when the hand of faith is weak, or the eye of faith is dim, it will go hard with us. When faith is dormant, the most insignificant stream will make us quiver and cry, 'I shall be drowned in the flood!' But when faith is dominant it fears not an ocean of difficulty or danger."

God has special words for you and me in Isaiah. The following verse has meant a great deal to me over the years: "'When you pass through the waters I will be with you; and through the rivers, they will not overthrow you.' What better assurance than that can the believing heart ask for? No matter how deep and wide and stretching, no matter how dark and foreboding the 'waters' of adverse circumstances may be to sight and sense, has not He who cannot lie declared, 'they *shall not* overthrow you.'"

Or, as the hymn puts it:

"'When through the deep waters I call thee to go,

The rivers of woe shall not thee overflow;

For I will be near thee, thy troubles to bless,

And sanctify to thee thy deepest distress.'"

How may we apply the actual crossing over by the people by faith? "They had the command of God for their warrant and the promise of God for their security, and these, when laid hold of, are sufficient to overcome all fears and danger."

Did you know that it is possible for two people to do the same thing but have a different result? The Egyptians certainly found that out. "The Israelites were acting according to God's will, the Egyptians were not." "The Egyptians perished because their movement forward was an act of presumption rather than an act of faith."

It has been rightly pointed out over the years that it is possible to get ahead of God, as well as being too far behind Him and His will!

Another application is that real faith helps Christians to pass through trials. In the passage in Exodus "we see how faith enables Israel to fearlessly venture themselves to enter a strangely formed valley between two mountain ridges of water, and to reach in safety the opposite shore. In like manner, a real faith in God will enable the Christian to pass through trials and troubles [that] destroy multitudes of people, and which will in due time" bring him or her "to the enjoyment of perfect bliss."

Moses is certainly blissful after passing through the waters. He is so joyful that he--and his sister Miriam and others--sing! He sings praise to God for the victory and deliverance God has provided.

There is another song that is sung by a group of God's people who have over and over again shown that "man's extremity is God's opportunity."

That group has been challenged by the Amazon and other bodies of water. They have been opposed--at times--by governments and other people.

Nearly each member has experienced a baptism of fire, but God has shown Himself faithful and given His peace that flows like a river--deeper and fuller every day.

I am writing of Wycliffe Bible Translators, who have translated God's Word into the mother tongues of people of over a thousand languages since the 1930's. I know a couple that God called from banking positions in Minnesota who are now living on the shores of Lake Victoria in Africa. God is doing exciting things in and through them as they trust Him for provision and opportunities and ministry.

We do not have to be mighty giants of faith to live for God today. But I would ask you what kind of challenges does God want you to face through faith in Him?

I hope you will join with Wycliffe Bible Translators around

the world who know and sing and live this song:

"Faith, mighty faith:
The promise sees and looks to God alone.
Laughs at impossibilities
And shouts, 'It shall be done.'
It shall, it shall be done.
Laughs at impossibilities
And shouts, 'It shall be done!'"

May God do so in your life as you trust Him as your great
Jehovah Who guides us!

Partitioned Portions of the Moses Wing:

- Section 19 –

"The Walls Fall"

By faith, the Israelites marched around the walls of Jericho for seven days, and the walls fell flat.
Hebrews 11:30   The Message

In 1989 the world witnessed the fall of the Berlin Wall. I don't know about you, but I never thought I would see that happen in my life time. What a joyous time it was, followed by the fall of the Soviet Union and freedom for many countries in Eastern Europe.

In Ephesians 2, Paul tells us that Jesus through the cross broke down the walls that divide us because of sin.

Then there is the passage of this chapter in Hebrews 11 and what it flashes back to in Joshua 5:13-6:21. Martin Marty once told the story of a pastor who wanted to check up on the Sunday School classes, to see how the teachers were doing. So he asked one student, "Who knocked down the wall of Jericho?" The boy replied, "It sure wasn't me, pastor."

Needless to say, the pastor was taken aback by this answer. He asked the boy's teacher, "Do you let your students get by with such things?" The teacher replied, "Look, reverend, Johnny is a good boy and doesn't lie. If he says he didn't do it, he didn't."

Even more upset, the pastor went to the church council. They met in private and reported back to the pastor with a written report that said: "After due consideration of the matter, we see no point in making an issue of the incident. The Board will pay for the damages to the wall and charge it off to vandalism."

In this chapter I am going to do what I can to keep a similar

131

situation from happening in your life and your church. The fall of Jericho's walls *is* an important incident. It is recorded in the Bible. It is further held up to us as an example of faith.

In this chapter we continue to be in the Hall of Faith. There is a partition in the Moses Wing. It is in that wing because it is connected with that period of time. It is partitioned, because it takes place after the death of Moses.

We read this Hall of Faith display in Hebrews 11:30, "By faith the walls of Jericho fell, after the people had marched around them for seven days."

Before looking more closely at this verse, we will flash back to the Old Testament passage to which it refers: Joshua 5:13-6:7.

In these verses, **instructions are given** from heaven to Joshua. Three principals are introduced in this story: two people and one place. The first person, or being, identifies Himself as the Commander of the Army of the LORD. Who is this? Let's look at the evidence. Joshua sees a man holding a sword. The man calls Himself the Commander of the Army of the LORD.

In response to this, Joshua falls facedown and worships the person. Joshua--a good Jew--would only do that if he thought he was in the presence of God.

Joshua calls Him "LORD" or in Hebrew, *Adonai*. Is Joshua mistaken? The Commander has an opportunity--as non-divine messengers do elsewhere in the Bible--to encourage Joshua to worship the Creator not creatures.

Instead, the Commander says, "Take off your sandals, for the place where you are standing is holy." Do you remember where else this has happened? When God speaks to Moses from the burning bush.

In Joshua 5 we have no One less than God, specifically the Second Person of the Trinity, the Son of God speaking to Joshua. You might remember that line from the hymn "For All the Saints" where we sing "Thou, LORD, their Captain, in the well fought fight."

Joshua is the second--and most visible to everyone else--person in this story. Joshua, whose name means "Yahweh is salvation" and is a form of the name Jesus.

Joshua, who had been Moses' lieutenant, his right hand man, now is the leader of Israel. Joshua gives ample proof that the choice of leader has been well made. He is ready to serve the LORD when he asks, "What message does my LORD have for His servant?"

He indicates an obedient faith by taking off his sandals, recognizing the holiness of God. Joshua will soon follow more instructions, but first the main location is introduced.

That of Jericho. One of the oldest cities in the world, there is archaeological evidence going back thousands of years before this episode.

It is the gateway to the Promised Land. It is the first city in that land for the Israelites.

The LORD gives Joshua instructions as to how Jericho will be taken. They are not your usual war preparations. It is clear that Jericho is not to be taken by human might or power, but by faith in the working of God's Holy Spirit.

Joshua faithfully passes along the instructions to the priests and people. The priests had been established by God when He had called the Israelite nation into being at Mount Sinai. The priests had earned their spurs of faith by the role they played in the crossing of the Jordan River. Now, they are called upon to play a major role in the taking of Jericho.

Joshua also gives instructions to the people as a whole. These people had wandered in the wilderness. Because of their parents' lack of faith, there was no one over 60, except for Joshua and Caleb.

The people will also be called upon to take part--by faith--in the taking of Jericho.

Next, **the instructions are carried out** in Joshua 6:8-19. The instructions are carried out by the priests as they sound the trumpets every day, with the ark of the LORD's covenant in procession. The instructions are carried out by the people as they circle Jericho once a day, not making any sound--not grumbling as their parents had, not second-guessing the strategy.

Before the big event, Joshua gives a warning. He tells them not to plunder. He tells them to spare Rahab and her family.

For now, you might be wondering about the ethics of all this--taking a city, killing people. In a few words, I do not think I can persuade you if you are not open to a reasonable explanation.

But for what it is worth, here it is. Elsewhere in the Bible, the Canaanites--the people inhabiting the Holy Land--are described as being exceedingly wicked. They deserve the punishment that comes upon them.

I might add that many years later in the Old Testament, the Israelites are treated similarly because of their disobedience to God's law.

On the positive side, this is the Promised Land for the nation of Israel. It is beyond the scope of this book to go into any applications of this to the 21st century Jewish state.

As far as Joshua 6 is concerned, please feel free to contact me (or Google the upcoming two words and Meredith Kline) about what is called "intrusion ethics."

Let's look now at the **God-given victory**, as it is recorded in Joshua 6:20&21. There is the noise of the trumpets and the roar of people's voices. Think about the roar at your favorite baseball or football team's stadium. There was a time less than ten years before the Berlin Wall feel when people outside the Gdansk, Poland, church shouted "Solidarity!" with such force that it could be heard in the nearby shipyard.

Whatever the physics of it, the walls of Jericho fall. This is followed by the fact that the people make a triumphal entrance and devote everything to the LORD. With that we return to **Hebrews 11:30**.

"By whose faith did the walls of Jericho fall down? Primarily by Joshua's; he believed and obeyed the divine instructions given him."

"But the people's faith was involved as well, for they carried out faithfully the instructions [that] Joshua communicated to them, until the city fell. But they could not see how it would fall; on the face of it, nothing could seem more foolish than for grown men to march round a strong fortress for seven days on end, led by seven priests blowing rams' horns."

It is hard to date the late Bronze Age Jericho, so it is hard to find visible evidence. "But the forces that operate in the unseen realm, such as the power of faith, cannot be dug up by the excavator's spade."

Joshua's powerful faith "is heard in his submissive reply to the divine messenger.... It is by the same faith that other Jerichos, both large and small can still be overthrown."

Jericho can be overthrown today if our faith includes **the five aspects of the Israelites' faith**. A. W. Pink writes about this faith. The first has to do with the *daring* of their faith. They were "in the enemy's territory, and victory or death were the only alternatives.

"There are three degrees of faith in the Christian life, each of which is needed. There is the faith, when as empty-handed beggars we come to Christ and accept him as our Lord and savior.

"There is a faith that counts upon God to fulfill his promises and undertake for us.

"There is also a faith that risks, that dares something for the

135

Lord. As the first modern era missionary to India--William Carey--once said, 'Ask great things of God; undertake great things for God.'"

The second aspect of the Israelites' faith is the *obedience* of their faith. "All concerned carried out the Lord's instructions to the letter." "Implicit obedience to the known will of God marked all Israel's arrangements for the siege of Jericho."

The third aspect is the *discipline* of their faith. "The soldier of Christ must be trained: faith must be disciplined: each one in the ranks of the Lord's hosts must learn there is 'a time to keep silent and a time to speak.'"

The fourth aspect is the *patience* of their faith. I "find it much harder to wait than I do to believe: that" could be one of the weakest parts of my "spiritual armor."

The fifth aspect is the *anticipation* of their faith. "The people shouted before the walls fell down--it was faith expecting the victory."

This anticipatory faith was found in a missionary by the last name of Moffat. He labored for a number of years among the Bechuana people and did not see a single person come to know the Lord.

"Some of his far-distant friends in England wrote him saying they wanted to give him a present and asked him to specify what it should be. He answered, 'A communion set.' Months later, when it arrived, more than a dozen converted Bechuanas sat down with him to remember the Lord's death!" That is anticipatory faith!

What are you anticipating by faith today? If it is not anything, then you need to search your heart and bring it before the LORD, asking Him to give you anticipatory faith for specific things.

All of Hebrews 11 and the whole of Joshua 6 have "been recorded for our learning. The walls of unbelief, superstition, and ungodliness, yield to no earthly armor and power.

"It is not by compulsion, nor by reasoning; it is not by weapons [that] this world supplies that these walls can be destroyed. It is by the Word of God, and by the Word declared in faith. Ministers and people---they who blow the trumpet, and also the people who are with them, are to be united together in the power of God.'

"Each of us is confronted with a Jericho: whether it be the pastor in the field of service where God calls him to labor; the Sunday School teacher in the call before him or her, or the individual Christian who is seeking to overcome some habit or attitude.

"Remember Joshua, and take courage! If there be the daring, the discipline, the obedience, the patience, and the expectation of faith, the victory is sure in God's appointed time."

"Awake, my soul, stretch every nerve,
And press with vigor on;
A heavenly race demands they zeal,
And an immortal crown."

- Section 20 -

"Faith for All, By All"

By an act of faith, Rahab, the Jericho harlot, welcomed the spies and escaped the destruction that came on those who refused to trust God.
Hebrews 11:31   The Message

In the previous chapter I told a story about how few people know, let alone understand, the story of the walls of Jericho. In this chapter we are going to consider a portion, a sub plot of that story.

Maybe fewer people know about this. But it is a story that needs to be told, to be heard and understood.

It is the story of Rahab, the story of her faith. Her Hall of Faith display is in the Moses Wing partitioned area, along with Joshua's faith and the fall of the wall of Jericho.

It is partitioned because, while it takes place during an era dominated by Moses, the actual events occur after the death of Moses. As far as Rahab goes, here is **an introduction and overview**. Let's listen to Rahab's story as it is found in the book of Joshua, and then examine some difficulties you and I might have with her inclusion in the Hall of Faith.

We first meet Rahab in Joshua 2, well before the walls of Jericho fall. Two spies have been sent by Joshua to look over the land, especially Jericho.

Through the providence of God they enter the house of Rahab the prostitute. The king of Jericho finds out about it, but Rahab enables the men to escape.

Before their departure, the spies agree to save Rahab and her family from the death and destruction that will soon overtake Jericho. In chapter 6, Joshua and the spies make good on their promise. Rahab and her family are spared and live in the midst of the Israelite nation overwhelming the city.

There are some difficulties here. This example of faith--the faith of Rahab--is the most surprising we have met so far in the Hall of Faith: Rahab, the harlot of Jericho.

You might be shocked or even offended that a prostitute is mentioned in a positive fashion in the Hall of Faith. Others have been scandalized--they have called her an innkeeper, anything but what she actually was.

But both the Old and New Testaments make it very clear by their words and contexts that Rahab was a prostitute. I emphasize *was*, because it is clear that God had been at work in Rahab's life before the two Israelites came to her home. Her faith in the God of Israel had already been awakened. The Holy One was speaking to her.

She was no longer debasing herself, though the label continued. As Charles Spurgeon writes, "Rahab's faith was a sanctifying one. Did Rahab continue a harlot after she had faith? No, she did not. I do not believe she was a harlot at the time the men went to her house, though the name still stuck to her, as such ill names will; but I am sure she was not afterwards, for Salmon the prince of Judah married her... You cannot have faith, and yet live in sin. To believe is to be holy. The two things must go together. That faith is a dead faith, a corrupt faith, a rotten faith, which lives in sin that grace may abound. Rahab was a sanctified woman. O that God might sanctify some that are here."

The second difficulty has to do with Rahab's lying to the king. This is a tough call. I remind you of Corrie ten Boom who, along with her family, lied to the Nazis to save the lives of Jews. Yet Arthur W. Pink tells us this lying indicates the imperfection of Rahab's faith. Fearful for the spies' lives, Rahab lies. The course she follows resembles the direction that Rebekah gave to her son

Jacob: in general, her intent was the fruit of great faith, for it respected the promise of God, but in the various details it cannot be approved.

"This is not for our imitation, yet it is for our instruction; and it shows us... that faith in the beginning has many weaknesses."

Pink continues on to write, "It is blessed to see that neither in our text nor in James 2:25 does the Holy Spirit make any reference [to] Rahab's failure; instead, in both places he mentions that which is praiseworthy, and to her credit. It is the very opposite with the malevolent world [that] is ever ready to overlook the good and reflect only upon the evil of an action performed by a child of God. It is a gracious spirit [that] throws the mantle of charity over the deformities and defects in a brother or sister in Christ, as it is honoring to God to dwell upon that which His Holy Spirit has wrought in them. If we were quicker to judge ourselves for our own sad failures, we would not be so ready to blaze abroad the faults of our fellows."

Now we can see the supposed difficulties of Rahab's Hall of Faith inclusion with new eyes. Let us turn to an examination of **Rahab's faith**--recognizing that at work in all of this is God--His sovereignty, His amazing grace and His power. Rahab's faith is remarkable when it is set in contrast to the Jews in the wilderness. "Hebrews 3:18 and 4:6 hold up to Christians... the behavior of the generations in the wilderness as a warning example. The man will come to grief who looks back, or stops his ears to God's instructions for the present time, and is not ready to receive the future from the hands of God in utter trust. Because of her faith Rahab the harlot was unlike the latter, and she did not meet with the destruction [that] came upon the disobedient inhabitants of Jericho."

This is all the more remarkable, when you consider Rahab's ethnic background. This may have been more of a scandal to the

Jews, than the two difficulties I have already written about.

Rahab is an Ammonite, a group of people that had become exceedingly wicked. So corrupt that they rightfully deserved God's judgment. In the midst of this deep darkness, one light shines--that of Rahab's faith.

With that we come to the place of beholding her faith in the context of the Fall of Jericho. Rahab's faith hearkens back to the operative definition given in Hebrews 11:1--"Now faith is being sure of what we hope for and certain of what we do not see."

Somehow, God awakens hope in Rahab. She comes to the place of putting her trust in the God of Israel--*before* the mighty city falls.

Think of it! "There were no Sabbaths observed in Jericho, there were no Scriptures available for reading, there were no prophets sounding forth messages from Heaven; nevertheless, Rahab was quickened into newness of life and brought into a saving knowledge of the true God." This is the power of God in action.

Rahab's faith in action is seen by her help to the spies. Her good works are the evidence before people that a spiritual principle has been communicated to her, the fruits of which justify or vindicate her profession, demonstrating that she is a member of 'the Household of Faith.'"

In "receiving the spies with peace" she makes it clear that she has a heart for the people of God, and is ready to do all in her power to help them.

What about the *nature* of Rahab's faith? It is a singular faith. The title of this chapter is "Faith By All, For All" and I will have more to say about that later. Right now I want to focus on the *singularity of her faith*.

"The city of Jericho [is] about to be attacked; within its walls there are hosts of people of all classes and characters, and they know that if their city should be set upon and stormed they would all be put to death. But strange to say, there is not one of them who repents of sin or who even asks for mercy, except this woman who had been a harlot. She and she alone was delivered, a solitary one among a multitude. Have you ever felt that it is a very hard thing to have a singular faith?"

I know I have. When I see people in the Anglican Church oppose bringing the Gospel to people of other faiths, I wonder about this.

So I ask again, "Have you ever felt that it is a very hard thing to have a singular faith? It is the easiest thing in the world to believe as everybody else believes, but the difficulty is to believe a thing alone, when no one else thinks as you think; to be the solitary champion of a righteous cause, when the enemy musters his thousands for battle. Now this is the faith of Rahab. She has no one who feels as she does, who may enter into her feelings and realize the value of her faith. She stands alone. It is a noble thing to be the lonely follower of despised Truth."

This faith does have its reward. Rahab does not perish with the disobedient. Further, she gets to dwell in Israel. "Thus, from being the slave of Satan she is adopted into the family of God; from being a citizen of [unbelieving] Jericho she is given a place in the congregation of the Lord."

Rahab dwells, or lives, in the midst of Israel. This is, I think, the key to **applying Rahab's story** to our lives. In actual space/time, Rahab lives in Israel. When the book of Joshua is written, she is still alive. We read in Joshua 6:25, "She lives among the Israelites to this day."

We learn even more from Rahab when we consider her place in salvation history. Rahab is one of the four women mentioned by name or reference in the genealogy of Jesus. The other three--Tamar, Ruth and Bathsheba were engaged in immorality or came from the wrong side of the tracks. The fifth--Mary--is an unwed mother to be.

Jesus, who on the human side of his roots is related to Rahab, shows a special heart for the down and out, the despised in society.

One of the knocks against Him that He wears as a badge of honor is that he is a friend of sinners, tax collectors and prostitutes.

One woman--probably a former prostitute--shows her gratitude to Jesus for having brought her the peace of forgiveness by anointing Jesus' feet with perfume, wets his feet with her tears, wipes them wither her hair, and kisses them. The Pharisee, in whose home Jesus is, recoils in horror. So Jesus tells a story with this point: "Her many sins have been forgiven."

What does this say to us? God can use anybody. It is a warning to the smug. Let us not be like the Pharisee, lest we learn that we are among the disobedient who will perish.

Let us also hear the joyful news that all are invited to put their trust in the true God. There is the opportunity for faith by all, because the invitation is for all to have faith. That does not mean that all will respond. But it *does* mean that all kinds of people from every race and walk of faith are called and chosen by God.

No matter what your background, you are invited to put your faith in Jesus Christ. Put that faith into action, be sure it is operative. Share that faith--in word and work.

Supplement to the Hall of Fame

- Section 21 -

"Hall of Shame"

*"We can't attack those people; they're way stronger than we are."
They spread scary rumors among the People of Israel."*
Numbers 13:31&32a   The Message

In this chapter we are going to step outside the Hall of Faith. We do so because an important event occurred in the history of Israel that is *not* recorded in Hebrews 11. It comes after the crossing of the Red Sea and before the taking of Jericho. It is not in Hebrews 11 because it is a story of *lack* of faith for all but two of the people.

The display can be found in a far corner of the grounds. It is no more than a run-down hut. The words over the creaking door say, "Hall of Shame." Once inside we enter the world of the Book of Numbers 13:1-14:38.

You may know that some sportscasters have their segments called "Hall of Shame," where they show the worst, poorest or tackiest events in the world of sports.

This Bible Hall of Shame is kind of like that. As we work our way through this passage, I think you will see the stark contrast between the unbelief here and the vibrant faith found in the Hall of Faith.

Numbers 13 begins well enough. In verses one through three, the LORD takes the initiative and commands Moses to send some men to explore the land of Canaan, the land given by the LORD to Israel. Moses is to choose one man from each of Israel's ancestral tribes.

Moses carries out the LORD's orders. In verse three, he picks them and prepares to send them.

The list is given in verses four through fifteen. The list of tribes and representatives will become members of the Hall of Shame, all except Caleb of Judah and Moses' lieutenant--Joshua-- who goes as Moses' representative.

In verses 17 through 20, Moses commissions the group. Moses poses the questions the scouting report is supposed to answer. After giving them the itinerary, he asks about the land: is it good or bad? That ties in with the soil: is it fertile or poor? Are there trees on it or not?

What about the people--are they strong or weak? Are the towns without walls or fortified?

In those days there were no satellites, planes or drones for reconnaissance, so people needed to check things out the old fashioned way!

Moses gives one final order, "Bring back some of the fruit of the land."

In Numbers 11:21-24 we read about the 40 day exploration. There is that number 40 again. It is found at many key turning points in the Bible and salvation history.

The scouts follow the route Moses had suggested. They also gather grapes, pomegranates and figs as Moses had ordered.

They cut off a branch bearing a single cluster of grapes. One writer notes that branches of grapes are still found in the Holy Land, "Weighing as much as eight, ten or twelve pounds, the grapes themselves being as large as our smaller plums."

Anyone going to Israel today, or seeing literature about Israel, knows that the symbol of the Israeli tourist Board is taken from this passage. It shows two men carrying a huge bunch of grapes on a pole.

In 26-33, we hear the report of the explorers.

First, they report on the land. It is "flowing with milk and honey." And they give proof of that, but... and here the story begins to go downhill. The people are huge and powerful. The cities are very large and fortified.

In verse 30 the minority report and recommendation are given by Caleb. He is a shining light in the midst of the gloom. He says: "we should go up and take possession of the land, for we can certainly do it."

Caleb says that we can do it, not because of our strength, but because God has called; God has given; and God will equip and enable.

The majority fights back in verses 31-33. They speak negatively and slap God in the face by so doing. They whine, "We can't attack, they are stronger than we are."

They tell falsehoods, giving propaganda to achieve their end. In verse 32 we read, "They spread among the Israelites a bad report about the land." It devours those who live in it. The people are huge. We are like grasshoppers by comparison.

In Numbers 14, the people rebel. We see the effect of a few on the many. As the Bible says, "A little yeast leavens the whole loaf." The many people are still responsible for their words and actions--they could have chosen to listen to and follow the minority report of Caleb and Joshua.

In verses one through four, there is open, verbal opposition. The people weep and whine. They grumble and say, "If only... we had died in Egypt or the desert." They are nominating themselves for the Hall of Shame!

They say, "Let's choose a leader!" With that the mutiny, the insubordination, comes into the open. By challenging Moses' authority, they are also rebelling against God Who had chosen Moses.

God's leaders respond in Numbers 14:5-9.   Moses and Aaron; Caleb and Joshua reply: the land is exceedingly good.   If the LORD is pleased with us, He will lead us into that land, and He will give it to us.

The godly leaders also give a solemn warning: do not rebel against the LORD.   Do not be afraid of the people.   Their protection is gone, but the LORD will be with us.   To God, the people of Palestine look a lot smaller than grasshoppers!   The leaders are trying to help the people see the situation from God's perspective, which is how church leaders should lead: do not focus on the problem; instead focus on the God who can do what seems impossible to us!

In Numbers 14:10-38, there is one crisis after another.   We read about God's response in verses ten through twelve.   The whole group talks about stoning Moses, Aaron, Caleb and Joshua.   Kill the messengers, God's messengers!

That is when the LORD steps in.   His glory appears in the tent of meeting.   The LORD speaks to Moses.   God says that "the people are treating Me with contempt."   In other words, Jehovah justly resents "conduct of the people as base contempt of His deity, and as utter mistrust of Him, not withstanding all the signs [that] He has done in the midst of the nation."

The LORD goes on to say that "they refuse to believe me." He says, "I will strike them with a plague."   He says, "I will make you, Moses, into a greater and stronger nation."

Instead of Moses saying, "That sounds good, LORD.   I'm tired of the hassle.   Do it," Moses intercedes for the people in Numbers 14:13-19.   In verses 13 through 16, Moses reminds God of the nation--what God has already done for Israel.   In 17 through 20, Moses reflects in prayer back to God Whom He is.

The LORD replies to Moses' prayer in Numbers 14:20-35. God does forgive the people, but as with any sins, there are still consequences. There will be judgment on the nation. All those over 20--except Caleb and Joshua--will die before entering the Promised Land. There is judgment on the explorers--all but Caleb and Joshua will die of a plague.

God does single out Caleb for praise in verse 24: "Because my servant Caleb has a different spirit and follows me wholeheartedly, I will bring him into the land he went to, and his descendants will inherit it."

What does it mean that Caleb has "a different spirit"? It means that his is "not the unbelieving, despairing, yet proud and rebellious spirit of the great mass of the people, but the spirit of obedience and believing trust, so that 'he followed Jehovah fully, followed him with unwavering fidelity.... God would bring him into the land in which he had gone.'"

For the fulfillment of the promise, all you need do is check out Joshua 14, which takes place 45 years after Numbers 13:14. We read in Joshua 14:13 that "Joshua blessed Caleb... and gave him Hebron as his inheritance."

The events recorded in Numbers 13&14 "form a grand turning-point in the history of Israel, in which the whole of the future history of the covenant nation is typically reflected. The constantly repeated unfaithfulness of the nation could not destroy the faithfulness of God, or alter His purposes of salvation. In wrath Jehovah remembers mercy; through judgment He carries out His plan of salvation, that all the world might know that no [person] is righteous before Him, and that the unbelief and unfaithfulness of men could not overturn the truth of God."

In this passage we learn many things. In this chapter I will share with you only three of the possible applications.

The first has to do with **the gravity of the sin of unbelief.** The sin of unbelief is very serious in God's eyes and therefore should be to us as well. We should shudder when we realize what our unbelief says about God.

It is as though we are slapping God in the face and saying, "You are not who you say you are and you cannot do what you say you can."

There are grave consequences to us--individually and as a church if we continue in the sin of unbelief. God's judgment will come upon us. We know not how or when, but it will.

In John 3:18--only two verses after the very famous verse of John 3:16, Jesus has some strong medicine for us: "Whoever believes in [the Son of God] is not condemned, but whoever does not believe stands condemned already because he has not believed in the name of God's one and only Son."

And on the night He establishes the Lord's Supper, Jesus tells His closest followers--and us--that the Holy Spirit will convict the world of three things, the first one being "in regard to sin, because men do not believe in me." That is found in John 16:8&9.

Out of all the sins Jesus could have picked out He chose one: unbelief, in this case not believing in Him. Moses and the other three godly leaders had to face unbelief during their time.

Is there a Moses reading this chapter, who but for him or her, God would have already come upon a city, state, or nation in wrath? Let's first put our own house in order and then intercede and pray for others.

I must ask this question: are we candidates for the Hall of Shame?

The second application of this passage has to do with **pleasing God.** In Numbers 14:8, there is a hint, a clue, pointer as to how we may leave the Hall of Shame hut and re-enter the Hall of Faith. That is when Joshua and Caleb say to the people, "*If the Lord is pleased with us,* He will lead us into the land."

If the LORD is pleased with us. Pleasing God. Making God smile.

How do we do that? He is not pleased when we rebel against Him. The letter to the Hebrews gives us at least two examples of pleasing the LORD. Enoch pleased God by how he lived his life. We read in the last part of Hebrews 11:5 that before Enoch was taken up to heaven, "He was commended as one who pleased God."

In Hebrews 13:16 we are told "to do good and to share with others, for with such sacrifices God is pleased."

Of course, what pleases God the *most* is our putting our full trust in Jesus Christ--for our lives and for the little things in life. Which leads me to the third application point:

God calls, gives, equips, and enables you! In Numbers 13:30, Caleb gives the minority report. He reminds the people that God has called, God has given, and God will equip and enable you.

If you would be known as a member of the Hall of Faith instead of the Hall of Shame, then realize and put into practice the facts that:

*God has called you to Himself;

*God has given you new life in Christ; and

*God will equip and enable you for whatever the future holds.

GALLERY OF FAITHFUL PEOPLE

*I could go on, but I've run out of time. There are so many more--
Gideon, Barak, Samson, Jephthah, David, Samuel, the prophets....*
Hebrews 11:32

Judges

- Section 22 -

Gideon

*All three companies blew the trumpets and broke the jars. They held
the torches in their left hands and the trumpets in their right hands,
ready to blow, and shouted, 'A sword for [the LORD] and for
Gideon!'"*
Judges 7   The Message

You might have heard of the group called the Gideons.
You have probably seen their literature. You might know a
Gideon, or be one yourself. You might have read part of a hotel
Gideon Bible, or might have a Gideon New Testament and Psalms
at home. Gideon Bibles are available in many hospitals and other
locations.

How did these people, so concerned about getting the Bible
into as many hands as possible around the world--how did they
come to call themselves Gideons? Why is their symbol that of a jar
with a flame coming out of it? I will give specific answers at the
end of this chapter.

For answers to these and other questions, we turn to the
seventh chapter of Judges. Here we have told the story that
provides Gideon's entrance into the Hall of Faith's "Gallery of
Faithful People."

In this chapter I will once again follow the pattern of

153

reading and telling the story; explaining the meaning of the story; and applying the story to our lives.

You may open your Bible to Judges 7 as I **tell the story**. Judges 7:1 provides background material. We are introduced to Gideon, the main character. In Judges 6, the LORD has called Gideon to overthrow the Midianites, who have been oppressing Israel.

One night, Gideon and his servants tear down the idolatrous altar of Ba'al and the Asherah pole that many Israelites had been worshiping--including his own family.

That act of tearing down the altar is what earns Gideon his nickname--"Jerub-Baal"--which means "let Baal contend." In other words, Gideon is contending against Baal on behalf of the LORD God.

The opponents--the opposition to God and therefore Gideon--are introduced in 7:1 as well. We read in 6:33 that "all the Midianites, Amalekites and other eastern peoples joined forces and crossed over the Jordan and camped in the valley of Jezreel."

In response to this invasion, Gideon summons the northern tribes of Israel. It is at this point that Gideon puts his two fleeces before the LORD and is convinced that the LORD will do as He promised--save Israel by Gideon's hand.

Now we are caught up and may continue the story in Judges 7. In verses two through eight, we find a very unique form of recruitment taking place. The LORD indicates to Gideon that the nature of the battle will be such that God will be glorified.

God gives Gideon instructions in verse three that are compatible with guidelines given in the book of Deuteronomy. He invites the fearful to leave. It does not help any army's morale to have cowards in the ranks.

But Gideon is probably stunned when he sees how many take him up on his offer. 22,000 out of 32,000 leave--more than two-thirds! This is even more amazing when we realize how large is the opposing army--it numbers around 135,000.

But a ten to one ratio--*against*--is not enough for God! God further reduces, He refines the number. Gideon's faith is tested as he prepares to follow God's orders.

Those orders, those specifications have to do with how each soldier drinks water from a river. Only 300 pass the test, those who "do not allow themselves time to kneel down and satisfy their thirst in the most convenient manner but simply take some water with their hands as they stand in their military outfit to strengthen themselves for battle, and they proceed without delay against the foe."

This makes the ratio of eastern people to Israelites 450 to 1! God is now ready to act. He promises in verse seven "with the three hundred men that lapped I will save you and give the Midianites into your hands."

Next, preparations are made in 7:9-18. Preparation is made in verses 9-14 through encouragement of Gideon by God. This comes by means of a dream that a Midianite had. Through God's direction, Gideon overhears the Midianite tell about the dream to a friend.

The friend understands the dream to mean that "God has given the Midianites and the whole camp into" Gideon's hands.

When Gideon hears this he worships God, then returns to the camp to prepare through the instructions to the troops. These are carried out as we read in verses 19 through 22.

After recruitment and preparations comes the battle. It takes place around midnight. The 300 divide into three groups of one hundred. At Gideon's signal the trumpets are blown and the jars are smashed. Then each one holds a trumpet in one hand and a torch in the other.

They blow on the trumpets and then shout, "A sword for

the Lord and for Gideon!" The soldiers do not move, "so that the Midianites necessarily think that [the Israelites] must be a numerous army advancing behind the torch-bearers."

The Midianites turn on themselves. Gideon and his 300 receive a complete victory from the LORD. That is something of Gideon's story.

What is the **meaning of the story**? One of the most important meanings has to do with the faith of Gideon. God requires a test of Gideon's faith, "by the purification of his army, that he might give the whole glory to God, and accept the victory over that great multitude from his hand alone."

The readiness with which Gideon reduces "his army to three hundred at the bidding of God reveals a faith equal to a strength of no ordinary faith."

Gideon's "whole conduct of the campaign against the Midianites reveals his faith."

Gideon learns the lesson that "God is not dependent upon numbers."

You may have wondered about the meaning of the dream the Midianite had. "The loaf of barley bread, which was the food of the poorer classes is to be regarded as strictly speaking the symbol of Israel, which was so despised among the nations."

How do we go about **applying the story** to our lives? I hope you have already been making some application for yourself.

We may apply the lesson that Gideon learns, namely that it is not how many of us there are, but whether we are doing the LORD's will. Are we truly gathered in the Name of Jesus? Then He has promised to be in our midst. What more does the Church need than the presence of Jesus? All blessings flow from that reality.

We may seek to have faith like Gideon's. In the face of seemingly insurmountable odds, he trusted in God instead of his own resources.

As we read and sing from the words of Jesus in Matthew 6:33, "Seek ye first the Kingdom of God and His righteousness, and all these things [--food, clothing, the necessities--] shall be added unto you."

We may respond to God's confirming His promises to us as He did to Gideon. "When Gideon heard the dream and its interpretation, he worshiped God." If Jesus is present, if we are doing God's will by seeking God's Kingdom and His righteousness, God will be confirming His promises to us in special, personalized ways.

As He does so, our appropriate response is to worship God. Worship is *always* the appropriate response to God. After surgery in 2007, for some years I received an envelope from the Mayo Clinic that I knew contained the results of a regularly taken test. I would say out loud before I opened the envelope, "Blessed be the Name of the LORD"--regardless of the results that I would find inside.

I promised near the beginning of this chapter that there would be an answer to the meaning of the Gideon's' symbol of a jar with fire. You have already heard about these two items in the story of the battle: the torches were carried inside the jars until the jars were broken. The fire symbolizes the word of God written-- the Bible--that the Gideons are so eager to share.

Each Gideon has come to know the transforming nature of the Bible through the power of the Holy Spirit. I think the jar speaks of the Gideons themselves. Christians are earthen vessels holding the glory of God.

What about the breaking of the jars? The Bible tells us that God will not despise a broken and contrite heart.

This has to do with shattered dreams, our plans instead of God's plans. As we are broken, God's light is able to shine that much more brightly. We are the clay, God is the potter. God is the One Who is re-making us into the image of His Son.

Here is one final question to answer: what is meant by the Sword of the LORD? For the answer, I turn to Hebrews 4:12 which says, "The word of God is living and active. It is sharper than any double edged sword, it penetrates even to dividing soul and spirit, joints and marrow; it judges the thoughts and attitudes of the heart."

The Bible--the Sword of the LORD--*is* dangerous: if you open it, read it and heed it, you will experience times of discomfort. But if you persevere in your Bible reading, you will realize that the sword is like the surgeon's blade--it cuts in order to bring healing.

That is what the modern day Gideons have learned. That is why they are so eager to get the Bible into the hands of people in every language possible. May we, like Gideon of long ago, entrust ourselves to God and allow Him to do the work of the Great Physician.

Jesus--the Great Physician--is the Word of God incarnate and the Bible is the word of God written, as we sing from the hymn penned by William W. How:

"O Word of God Incarnate, O wisdom from on high,

O truth unchanged, unchanging, O light of our dark sky,

We praise Thee for the radiance that from the hallowed page,

A lantern to our footsteps, shines on from age to age."

Samson: "Declaration of Dependence"

LORD God! "Oh, please, look on me again,
Oh, please give strength yet once more.
God! With one avenging blow let me be avenged
On the Philistines for my two eyes!"
Judges 16

Please read what John wrote to Abigail about the momentous event: "I am well aware of the toil and blood and treasure that it will cost us to maintain this declaration, and support and defend these states. Yet through all the gloom I can see rays of ravishing light and glory. I can see that the end is worth more than all the means."

Those words were penned by John Adams to Abigail his wife on the passing of the Declaration of Independence. That Declaration, written mostly by Thomas Jefferson, is a declaration of both <u>in</u>dependence *and* <u>de</u>pendence.

Jefferson himself depended a great deal on pastors. He borrowed heavily from "the phraseology of popular sermons of the day."

In order to get the Declaration passed, there was a great dependence on other humans. The Delaware delegation was deadlocked, so a rider was sent to Dover to fetch the third delegate, Caesar Rodney, who voted in favor of the Declaration.

Dependence upon God is heard in the text itself: "Endowed by the Creator," and "with a firm reliance on the protection of Divine Providence" are two examples.

The notion that all men are created equal, indicates both dependence on God and independence from tyrannical rulers. "It is difficult for us, with ten generations of democracy behind us, to

159

appreciate just how radical were the words of the Declaration of Independence that 'all men are created equal!'"

This document, which is celebrated every July Fourth, has two sides to it. It is a declaration of independence from King George. It is also a declaration of *dependence*--on one another and God. The rallying cry of that time resounds to our day, "No King but Jesus!"

This is a written declaration of both independence and dependence, written more than 240 years ago.

A little over three *thousand* years ago, there was a spoken declaration of independence and dependence. It was spoken by Samson.

The Philistines had oppressed the Jews for 40 years when Samson was born. Samson is another member of the Gallery of Faithful people in the Hall of Faith.

His mother shows a healthy faith that depends upon God. The angel of the LORD appears to Manoah and his wife. When Manoah the husband realizes this he wails, "We are doomed to die! We have seen God."

His wife, however, calmly points out that "if the LORD had meant to kill us, He would not have accepted a burnt offering and grain offering from our hands, nor shown us all these things or now told us this."

It is clear that God has something special in store for Samson. Samson, however, turns out to be especially difficult. He is "petulant and vindictive; his action [is] determined not, as is the case of the other judges-- the desire to deliver Israel from the oppressor--but to avenge wrongs inflicted upon himself."

Samson gets himself into a heap of trouble, yet God chooses to grant him some portion of the Spirit of the LORD. Ultimately, Samson is captured by the Philistines, who gouge out his eyes and bind him with shackles.

At this point in his life, **Samson is dependent on humans** because he is a prisoner and is blind. In Judges 16:23-25 the emphasis is on Samson the prisoner. He has lost his freedom. Hebrews 11:36 speaks of people being chained and put in prison.

The rulers of the Philistines get together to celebrate their catch of Samson. They prepare to offer a great sacrifice to Dagon, a fish deity whose shape resembles "the body of a fish with the head and hands of a man."

The Philistines claim that their God has delivered their enemy--Samson--into their hands.

When the people see Samson, they praise Dagon and say, "Our god has delivered our enemy into our hands, the one who laid waste our land and multiplied our slain."

While they party, little realizing their impending doom, they call for Samson to come from prison and make him perform like some freak side show.

In verses 26&27, we see Samson the blind man. He is dependent on another person to get around. He asks the servant to put him between the two pillars that provide the main support for the temple. Samson has an idea, which will soon become clear.

In verses 28-30, **Samson's dependence upon God is seen.** Samson acknowledges his dependence in verse 28. Psalm 82 had not been written at the time of Samson, but I find verse 7 quite appropriate: "My salvation and my honor depend on God; he is my mighty rock, my refuge."

Some of that is echoed, albeit with mixed motives, as Samson prays, "O Sovereign LORD, remember me. O God, please strengthen me just once more, and let me with one blow get revenge on the Philistines for my own two eyes."

In verses 29&30 Samson is set free. He braces himself against the two key pillars holding up the temple of Dagon. He bows his back and bends the pillars. Samson yells his declaration of independence, "Let me die with the Philistines!"

This is not a suicidal death wish. In this action, which literally brings the house down, the LORD proves to the Philistines that the shame of Samson's sin is "taken from him, and that the Philistines have no cause to triumph over him."

Samson's words are no more suicidal than those of Patrick Henry, "Give me liberty or give me death!"

Samson's "last act is his greatest and best, furnishing the strongest evidence of his faith in God."

It is a declaration of both independence and dependence.

When it comes to application let's first consider **dependence**. I realize that dependence does not come easily to most of us. I remember once talking with a senior citizen. She was talking of her eye problems and financial difficulties.

I said to her, "It's frustrating having to depend on others, isn't it?" She responded, "You've got that one right!"

Part of growing old gracefully involves being willing to depend on others and on God. I emphasized to that senior citizen that she needed to allow other people to receive the blessing of helping her.

Jesus says, "It is more blessed to give than to receive." If we are not willing to be on the receiving end once in a while, we keep other people from being blessed.

Next, I want to write something about **the wrong kind of dependence**. We know about clinging vines: people who drain you emotionally and otherwise by taking, taking, taking.

In those cases, the healthiest and best way to deal with the person is to lovingly help them stop being leeches.

Then there is the dependence on alcohol and other drugs. There are other kinds of addictions as well. They become crutches, creating even further problems.

Throughout the country are Celebrate Recovery groups that enable you to break free of addiction and be freely dependent upon God.

Even here, there is the need for a declaration of dependence. First, recognizing the dependency. Second, recognizing our dependence upon God to deliver us and be our strength. Third, a healthy interdependence with those who are going through the same process. And the list goes on.

It is not only the addicted person who is a prisoner, who can be blind to his or her problem. We are all prisoners to sin. If we do not acknowledge that, then we show our blindness as well.

Jesus says, "If you were blind, you would not be guilty of sin; but now that you claim you can see, your guilt remains."

We are *all* prisoners of sin. Only God can declare us and make us free from that bondage through Christ's work on the cross.

We are all spiritually blind. Only Jesus Christ--the light of the world--can help us see.

One of my favorite hymns by Charles Wesley puts it very well—

"Long my imprisoned spirit lay,
Fast bound by sin and nature's night.
Thine eye diffused a quickening ray;
I woke, the dungeon flamed with light.
My chains fell off, my heart was free:
I rose, went forth, and followed thee."

Let us declare our dependence upon God. As we do so, we will hear God's declaration of independence: "You shall know the truth. And the truth shall make you free."

Jesus is the Way, the Truth and the Life. He has made a

way to declare us free from our sinful nature--by His work on the cross.   He is the Truth--no one comes to God the Father except through Him.   He is the Life--through his death we have the offer of abundant life now and eternal life forever.

Prophets

- Section 24 -

Samuel: "A Mother's Faith"

"Oh, [LORD]-of-the-Angel Armies,
If you'll take a good, hard look at my pain,
If you'll quit neglecting me and go into action for me
By giving me a son,
I'll give him completely, unreservedly to you.
I'll set him apart for a life of holy discipline."
1 Samuel 1   The Message

I have had the privilege of preaching from this passage several times on Mother's Day. This is a day set aside to honor those who have received the high calling of motherhood.

What better way to honor mothers, and to instruct the rest of us, than by considering the faith of a woman who lived in Bible times.

In this chapter we begin the portion of the "Prophets" section of the Gallery of Faithful People.   He is considered to be the first of the Bible's prophets, at least in the listings of the Bible books when referred to ("from Samuel onwards").   The two books of Samuel are also listed under the history section of the Old Testament.

Samuel exercised priestly functions and anointed the first two kings of Israel.

How did he come to be?   Who was his mother?   It is quite a story.   There are similarities between the mothers of John the Baptist and Jesus.   Each of these mothers knew the pain of separation at some point. In this chapter we will consider a mother's faith, the faith of Hannah, the mother of Samuel.

165

In Hannah's case, there is an added agony--even before the birth of her first child. It is the agony of infertility and the intense feeling of failure that that brings.

Please read 1 Samuel 1:1-8 for yourself. In this section **the situation is presented**.

The first two verses introduce the parents-to-be. The father's name is Elkanah. Without going into a detailed explanation of how, I will simply let you know that Elkanah comes from a family of priests.

The meaning of his name indicates this background: "the man whom God has bought or acquired."

The mother-to-be is named Hannah, which means "God is gracious." Hannah will be finding out just how gracious God is. But first there is trouble and turmoil.

The problem is introduced in verses two and three. You see, Elkanah has another wife. The Bible does not condone bigamy or polygamy. As a matter of fact there is story after story that indicate heartaches involved in multiple marriages. But we are not to make any connections between the situation in the Bible and the twisted and horrendous practices that have been exposed in some modern day cults.

Returning to the story, the biggest area of conflict between the two wives--Peninnah and Hannah--is that of children. Peninnah has children, while Hannah does not.

The priests are introduced in verse three, when Elkanah takes his family to worship the LORD Almighty in Shiloh. The older priest's name is Eli. His sons' names are Hoophni and Phineas.

Elkanah gives Hannah a double portion of food and expresses his love for her, though the fact remains that he has another wife who has given birth. We read that the LORD had closed Hannah's womb. That may be difficult to understand, or even accept, but the LORD does do that sometimes.

When He does it, He always has a purpose, even if that purpose is not readily understandable. Hannah had no recourse to medical help for infertility in those days.

At a minimum, it causes her to be dependent on God, as Abraham's wife Sarah had been, and as John the Baptist's mother Elizabeth would be.

If this reality is not agonizing enough, Penninah hassles Hannah. Penninah provokes her, rubbing in the fact of Hannah's childlessness.

How brutal some people can be. We need to pray to be delivered from insensitivity--whether it is pre-meditated or unthinking. We know that for Penninah, it is pre-meditated. We read that she does this in order to irritate Hannah.

And Penninah *does* get under Hannah's skin. To the point that Hannah trembles, weeps and cannot eat.

And there is Elkanah. When I first came to this passage, I thought that he was being loving again--this time with his words. And, maybe by his own lights he was.

But I have been since informed by ladies that it is just the opposite and that Elkanah's remarks would be heard by Hannah as insensitive and very chauvinistic. Here is how *The Message Bible* puts it-- "'Oh, Hannah, why are you crying? Why aren't you eating? And why are you so upset?'" Here comes the crushing egotistic phrase-- "'Am I not of more worth to you than ten sons?'"

But Hannah is at the point of desperation. She does eat something. She does not lash out at her husband. Instead, she takes her overwhelming burden to the LORD in prayer.

The prayer is offered and a vow made in verses nine through 18. We see that Hannah takes action--she goes to the temple and weeps before the LORD.

167

Her prayer is one of honesty. She does not pull any punches. She is honest with the LORD about her bitterness of soul.

Her prayer includes a vow: "'LORD, if you listen to me and give me a son, I will give him back to you for a lifetime.'"

Hannah is praying with great intensity. She is praying in her heart, and her lips are moving, but no sound is coming out. This might be something like what the Apostle Paul writes about in his letter to the Romans--prayers that are groans and are too deep for words.

It is at this time that the elderly priest takes notice of her. Eli sees her haggard face, with its voiceless moving mouth and concludes that she is drunk based on the external evidence. He encourages her to stop getting drunk.

To his credit, Eli does listen to Hannah's response. She clarifies the situation by telling Eli that she is pouring her soul out to the LORD, praying in great anguish and grief.

Eli blesses Hannah and offers a prayer for her. This encourages Hannah, whose condition improves. She thanks Eli, has something to eat and is no longer depressed.

Nothing has happened. Hannah is still childless. So why the change? Hannah has received assurance from a representative of God. Hannah is still childless. Hannah's condition improves because she has faith that God will hear and act.

That indeed is the case, as we read in verses 19 through 28 where

The prayer is answered and the vow is kept. First, we see that God answers Hannah's prayer. She conceives and gives birth to a son. She names him Samuel, which sounds like the Hebrew for "heard of God." Imagine her joy and the confirmation of her faith.

Next, Hannah asks to be excused from the annual trip to Shiloh. Elkanah shows his love by saying, "Do what you think is best," and, "Be sure to keep your vow."

Hebrew mothers usually took around three years to wean their babies. So Hannah delights in her toddler. When the time does come, Hannah makes good on her vow.

She takes little Sam to the temple of the LORD. She dedicates him to the LORD. She presents Samuel to Eli.

First, she identifies herself to him and tells how God as answered prayer. Then she gives Samuel to the LORD. "For his whole life he will be given over to the LORD."

Samuel remains and worships the LORD. He is probably brought up on a day to day basis by one or more of the women at the house of the LORD, with Eli and his sons overseeing his training.

Samuel gets to see his family at least once a year and he probably travels to his home town on a regular basis as he gets older.

The LORD honors a mother's faith by providing a person who will be an important leader of Israel. An entire sermon series could be given on Samuel, who is prophet, priest and king-maker.

He is used by God at a pivotal time in salvation history--the establishment of royalty in the nation of Israel.

But in this chapter, the focus is on Samuel's mother and her faith.

I turn now to some **application** based on this true story. What can we learn from this expression faith? Hannah's faith is seen in many ways:

*How she is willing to turn to God and be open to Him about her hurt and her wish.

*Her willingness to give her first born to the LORD.

*And then her actually doing that--giving over her son to the care of priests.

In this true story, we also learn of God's care, as He hears Hannah's prayer, and answers it;

*as he honors her commitment by giving her more offspring; and

*as God lovingly works all this into His larger plan--how He plans to use Samuel.

What is our response to all of this?   The faith of Hannah is an example to us all: man or woman; whether a mother or not.

*How do we respond to heartache and hope deferred? With bitterness that does not turn to God?   Or with honesty and openness looking to God for help?

*Are you willing to trust God that He *does* have a purpose in everything He has brought into your life?   Can you trust Him enough to tell Him you are hurting, even angry at Him?   He has big shoulders.

Are you able to trust that God is working your life into part of His larger quilt of salvation?

*If you are not able to trust Him for these things, then will you take the first step and tell God that you are struggling and ask Him to help you trust Him?

*If you are already experiencing something like Hannah's faith, blessed are you.   May you not rest on your laurels, but press on: seeking to know Christ ever more deeply.

"Tho' He giveth or He taketh,
God His children ne're forsaketh;
His the loving purpose soley
To preserve them holy."

- Section 25 -

Samuel and David:

"Faith's Perspective"

The LORD told Samuel, "Looks aren't everything. Don't be
impressed with his looks and stature. I've already eliminated him.
[The LORD] judges persons differently than humans do. Men and
women look at the face; [the LORD] looks into the heart."
1 Samuel 16:7   The Message

"You can't judge a book by its cover."   "Don't judge a book
by its cover."   You have probably heard that saying when it comes
to things or people.   Maybe you have been on the receiving end of
someone sizing *you* up incorrectly.

There have been times when I have looked at someone and
formed the wrong impression of him or her.   Sometimes first
impressions are accurate.   Sometimes they are not.

In this chapter's passage, Samuel learns not to judge a book-
-or, in this case, a brother--by its cover, by appearance, by first
impression.   Samuel learns the importance of listening to God
rather than what his eyes tell him.   He learns faith perspective.

Perspective is what this passage is all about.   My little
dictionary defines perspective as "the appearance of objects as
determined by their relative distance and positions."   Also as a
"sense of proportion."

I learned something about perspective while on a train trip
in June of 1979 from Toronto to Calgary, and then a bus from
Calgary to Vancouver.

I realized how one's position affected what one saw.   Trees
that towered when one looked at them from below, looked very
small when seen from half way up a mountain.   The mountains

themselves looked small from far away, yet took up the whole view when right next to me.

Perspective--the position from which we view the world-- is very important. A mountain of problems might really be a molehill when seen from the proper perspective.

Or there may well be a granite obstacle of thousands of feet. But have you looked carefully? Is there not a tunnel through which you can travel to the other side?

Perspective is important in one's faith life. How we view the world and God's Kingdom. An example of faith's perspective is found in 1 Samuel 16:1-16.

In verse one we learn of faith's perspective. It is provided by God. The LORD speaks to Samuel. I cannot emphasize that enough.

Samuel the prophet has been mourning the fall of Saul. Samuel had anointed Saul as the first king of Israel. But he had disobeyed God.

God had rejected Saul. This is a grave matter--to be rejected by God after having been given the opportunity to serve Him.

Saul had his opportunities to be the leader of God's people. Saul had literally and physically been head and shoulders above everyone else.

But God says to Samuel, "It is time to move on, to anoint the next king."

God provides instructions for Samuel to follow by faith.

God gives Samuel specific instructions as to how to find the next king of Israel. He is to go to the family of Jesse. We read about Jesse's grandparents in the book of Ruth--the book just before First Samuel.

Jesse and his family live in Bethlehem, which we know

would become the birthplace of Jesus the Messiah, our Lord and King.

God explains the anointing process and meaning. After God speaks to Samuel He sends Samuel to Jesse of Bethlehem.

But notice that God does not tell Samuel everything. He tells him enough for Samuel to know that he is headed in the right direction. He knows that one of the sons of Jesse in Bethlehem is to be anointed king--but not which one.

God is testing, stretching the faith of Samuel, helping his perspective to be keener and truer.

The test comes in verse two. In verses two and three, Samuel challenges the LORD. Saul's emotional troubles have already started and Samuel is aware that Saul would probably kill him if he finds out what he is doing. Samuel fears a man and raises a concern.

God responds and provides a way, a tunnel through the mountain. He instructs Samuel to offer a sacrifice and invite Jesse's family.

This is not lying or using a falsehood. Samuel is a priest as well as a prophet. And it is during a time when there is neither a tabernacle nor a temple. So, he offers sacrifices wherever he goes.

Samuel, as he has consistently done through his life, gains the perspective of faith and he acts upon it by going to Bethlehem.

In verses 4 and 5a when Samuel rides into town, the leaders tremble. That is because "the prophet Samuel [is] frequently in the habit of coming to one place and another, for the purpose of reproving and punishing wrong-doing and sin."

I am reminded of part of a tongue in cheek description of the perfect pastor that says, "He speaks out against sin, but never hurts anyone's feelings."

Samuel does not always come in peace. So the trembling

leaders heave a sigh of relief when Samuel indicates that he has come to offer a sacrifice.

With that we come to verses 5b through 13. Jesse and his sons are invited to a feast. Little do they know that it will be a coronation banquet!

Jesse's sons are brought before Samuel. Samuel thinks the beauty contest is over with the first entry. He looks at Eliab and is sure he is to be the king. Samuel lapses into a human, non-faith perspective. God had said *He* would tell Samuel who the proper choice is.

So, God speaks again to Samuel in verse seven, which is the key to this whole passage and teaches us about faith's perspective: "Do not consider his appearance or his height, for I have rejected him. The Lord does not look at the things man looks at. Man looks at the outward appearance, but the Lord looks at the heart."

The Lord calls Samuel--and us--to not look at people and events from a worldly point of view.

Whenever we are in the midst of a presidential campaign, television advertisements tell us one thing and another about style and substance. Should that matter?

What does the United States constitution say about the qualifications for president: he or she must be at least 35, a natural born citizen, and have lived in the United States for the last 14 years. That's it.

There certainly are intangible questions such as, "Is this person a good administrator? How does he respond in a crisis situation? Can she lead?" "Does he plan on keeping his oath to uphold and follow the U. S. Constitution?

As voters, we are not to look on the outward appearance. Instead, as best we can, we decide based on what we think motivates this person, what direction he will lead us, and whether we agree with that direction.

Peter Marshall was a chaplain of the United States senate. His wife was Catherine Marshall, who wrote such books as *A Man Called Peter* and *Christy*.

Peter Marshall wrote the following prayer for election day. It is found in *Hymns for the Family of God*:

"Lord Jesus, we ask Thee to guide the people of this nation as they exercise their dearly bought privilege of franchise. May it neither be ignored unthinkingly nor undertaken lightly. As citizens all over this land go to the ballot boxes, give them a sense of high privilege and joyous responsibility.

"Help those who are about to be elected to public office to come to understand the real source of their mandate--a mandate given by no party machine, received at no polling booth, but given by God; a mandate to represent God and truth at the heart of the nation; a mandate to do good in the name of Him under whom this country was established.

"We ask Thee to lead our country in the paths where Thou wouldst have her walk, to do the tasks which Thou hast laid before her. So may we together seek happiness for all our citizens in the name of Him who created us all equal in His sight, and therefore brothers. Amen."

"The Lord does not look at the things man looks at." Elsewhere God says, "My thoughts are not your thoughts. Neither are your ways my ways, declares the Lord."

Samuel is learning an important lesson, even as the nation is on the verge of having a new king anointed.

Seven sons are brought before Samuel. None of them is God's chosen. Someone with merely a human perspective might

175

well throw up his hands and say, "That's it! God made a mistake. What do I do now?"

Instead, Samuel remembers the tunnels the LORD has already provided. He asks, "Are these all the sons you have?" Jesse admits that there is one more--the youngest, who is tending sheep.

This will be David--called from shepherding sheep to shepherding the nation of Israel. Just as the Roman Lucius Quintus Cincinnatus--after whom Cincinnati is named--is called from his plow to lead Rome--so David is called from his faithful, obedient shepherding of the sheep to lead Israel, as a man after God's own heart.

A word may be said here about David. He does sin--in big ways--later on in life. He falls away from God. But the difference between Saul and David is that David repents. He changes his mind, he recognizes that he has sinned against God, he turns from the sin and turns toward God.

He has the perspective of faith. He trusts that God will forgive him. Another prophet--Nathan--confronts him with his sin and David repents and is willing to bear the consequences of his sin.

But returning to this chapter's story, we see David brought to Samuel. David is handsome, but God does not disqualify him for that. The LORD grants Samuel the perspective of faith to see that David is the one. So Samuel anoints the red-headed David.

After David is anointed, two things happen: the Spirit of the LORD comes upon him; and he returns to shepherding his sheep, before being called to minister to troubled King Saul with his music.

"After receiving the Spirit of the Lord in consequence of the anointing, David leaves the further development of the matter to the Lord in childlike submission, assured that he would prepare

176

and show him the way to the throne in his own good time."

And that he would. David has had such an impact upon ancient and modern Israel, that the symbol on the Israeli flag is the Star of David.

I have been to that land. I have seen many Star of David flags on the top of Mount Massadah as soldiers are inducted into the military.

When I was in Israel, I took several half day, a full day, and one overnight bus tour. Usually the guides had agreements with merchants to stop so tourists would by their wares. Such was the case on the way to Bethlehem, when the bus stopped by prior arrangement at a souvenir store.

I was furious. I had not come all this way to look at trinkets. I wanted to be in the town where Jesus had been born. It all seemed so tacky and petty.

I stomped through and out of the store onto a patio. I was consumed with my anger. I built a molehill into a mountain.

But then I realized the answer was in the hills, the open hills of which this patio provided an ideal view.

I began to look at the hills around Bethlehem with faith's perspective. I imagined the love story of Ruth and Boaz, the grandparents of Jesse.

With the perspective of faith, I saw David--in obedience to his father and his God--shepherding the sheep.

I saw other shepherds on another glorious night--fearing the angels and beholding Christ the King--the baby Jesus who grew up and now sits forever on the throne of David.

When I was called to the bus, I was content. What had been a problem became--with the perspective of faith--the best part of my trip to Bethlehem.

That is what having faith's perspective can do. A

perspective from God and a trust in Him that He will see you through.

David was a shepherd. Jesus is the Good Shepherd. At the beginning of Psalm 23, David has one sheep bragging to another sheep about his shepherd: "The Lord is *my* shepherd, I shall not want."

"Savior, like a shepherd lead us,

Much we need Thy tender care;

In Thy pleasant pastures feed us,

For our use Thy folds prepare.

Blessed Jesus, blessed Jesus,

Thou hast bought us, Thine we are."

- Section 26 -

Elijah: "Life-Giving Faith"

"This is the word of the [LORD] of Israel: 'The jar of flour will not run out and the bottle of oil will not become empty before [the LORD] sends rain on the land and ends this drought.'"
1 Kings 17   The Message

If any of you have lived through a drought, you have become aware of many things. You realize the necessity of water and how the price of food goes up.

There is usually heat and (sometimes) humidity that go along with the drought. This makes us aware of our need to have temperatures within a certain range in order to be at our healthiest.

Have you noticed when you go outside on a 95 degree, 50 percent humidity day that it is hard to breathe?

For some people with respiratory problems, the heat and humidity can be more than a nuisance. People can be hospitalized, and even die from heat.

Drought makes us aware that food and weather are life and death issues. We need bread, the staff of life. We need to be able to breathe, the stuff of life.

The Bible speaks of such issues. It does so because it tells the story of people like you and me. We are grateful that the Bible does not stop there, but shows how God cares for people during hard times.

One such true story is found in 1 Kings 17. Let's look at verses 7 through 16 where we learn of **the bread of life**, of a sustaining miracle. We first meet Elijah. He is one of the great prophets that we meet in the historical books of the Bible's Old Testament. He is not what is called a "writing prophet"--one who has a book or two in the prophetical section of the Old Testament.

179

In an upcoming chapter you can read about Daniel, who was a writing prophet.

Elijah is a prophet of the LORD. That is why we are looking at this story--because the writer of Hebrews speaks of the faith of the prophets in the Hall of Faith's Gallery of Faithful people. In the next chapter I will look at Elijah's power encounter with the priests of a false God.

Elijah is a prophet of the LORD who has spoken the word of the LORD against Ahab. Elijah brings about the drought. He says, "There will be neither dew nor rain in the next few years at my word."

He goes to a solitary place, to the Kerith Ravine east of the Jordan, until the brook runs dry.

Then the LORD instructs Elijah to go to Zarephath, which is on the Mediterranean coast between Tyre and Sidon in what today is Lebanon. He is instructed to find a widow, who will supply him with food. He meets her at the city gate and asks for some bread and water.

Her response indicates at least two things: the drought has extended beyond the borders of Israel and thus King Ahab's disobedience is causing many to suffer; and, second, the woman, though a non-Jew, has some faith in the God of Israel.

Elijah asks her to take a step of faith. There are words of assurance as he says to her, "Do not fear." There are words of action when he says, "Go and do as you've said." There are words of addition when he says, "Make a cake of bread for me."

Elijah is not being selfish, but calling upon her to act in faith and to show that the first fruits belong to God.

The woman accepts the words as from the LORD. She accepts the words of promise and she acts in obedience.

Do you notice how God has set things up for mutual dependence, for interdependence? The woman has the bread and oil, meager though the amount is. Elijah has the word from the LORD that a miracle will occur. They are dependent upon each other and both are dependent upon God.

The widow "gives up the certain for the uncertain, because she trusts the word of the Lord, and receives the reward of her believing confidence in the fact that during the whole time of the drought she suffers no lack of either meal or oil."

Elijah has come because the LORD has commanded him to do so. He is sent to this particular widow in order to strengthen and increase her faith. The miracle of the meal and oil is "a preparatory means of quieting her spiritual need as well."

You have heard about the sustaining miracle, the provision of the bread of life. Listen now to the resurrection miracle, **the breath of life**, as it is reported in verses 17-24.

Sometime later the son of the widow stops breathing and dies. The widow confronts Elijah. It is the anguished cry of a mother. She wonders if God is punishing her. To his credit, Elijah does not put her down or lecture her.

But because you might be wondering about the same subject, please let me assure you that, "like the blindness in the case of the man born blind in John 9 [whom Jesus heals], the death of this widow's son is not sent as a punishment for particular sins, but is intended as a way to show her the works of God... in order that she might learn that the Lord is not merely the God of the Jews, but of the Gentiles also."

Once again, Elijah is asking her to give up something. First, it was her right to the first bread cake. Now, it is to entrust her dead son to his care.

Elijah takes action. He takes the son to the upper room where he is staying. Then he cries out to the LORD. Elijah's prayer is not a reproach of God, but is expressive of compassion and "the deepest lamentations, which springing from living faith, pours out the whole before God in the hour of distress, that it may appeal to him the more powerfully for his aid.

"The meaning [of the prayer] is, 'you, O Lord my God, according to your grace and righteousness cannot possibly leave the son of this widow in death.' Such confident belief carries within itself the certainty of being heard. The prophet therefore proceeds at once to action, to restore this boy to life."

Elijah's prayer is heard and the boy is restored to his mother. Her faith in God is restored and deepened. "Through this miracle, in which Elijah shows himself as the forerunner of Him who raises all the dead to life, the pious woman is mightily strengthened in her faith in the God of Israel. She now not only recognizes Elijah as a man of God but perceives that the word of the Lord in his mouth is truth, by which she confesses openly her faith in the God of Israel as the true God."

There is the resurrection miracle, through the breath of life. There is the sustaining miracle, through the bread of life. Have you noticed the other miracle?

It is the miracle of faith. With that we come to **direct application**. We are talking here about faith. It is this sort of faith that we are to have in Christ the bread of life. Jesus fed thousands in His lifetime. Even more importantly he had these words to say, "I am the bread of life" and "man does not live by bread alone, but by every word that proceeds from the mouth of the Lord."

The miracle of faith involves faith in Christ's Spirit, Who is the breath of life. The New Testament records examples of people being raised from the dead. Jesus calls Lazarus back to life, and gives an only son back to his widowed mother.

In the Book of Acts, we behold Peter calling Tabitha back to life and Paul restoring Eutychus who had fallen out of a window.

For us, we have a need for the breath of God, the Holy Spirit in our lives. He gives us power to love and to serve. He gives us power to love and to serve.   He gives us insight to understand and apply the Word of God.   The bread of life and the breath of life-- we need them both.

> "Breathe on me, breath of God,
> Fill me with life anew,
> That I may love what thou dost love,
> And do what Thou wouldst do."

- Section 27 -

Elijah: Power Encounter

All the people saw it happen and fell on their faces in awed worship, exclaiming, "[The LORD] is the true God! [The LORD] is the true God!"
1 Kings 18

In the previous chapter we considered the miracles of bread, life and faith as we learned of the prophet Elijah's sustaining the small supply of meal and oil for a widow, as well as his raising the widow's son from the dead. We beheld the widow's faith in both instances and were reminded that we are to put our faith in Jesus who is both the Bread of life and the Resurrection and the Life.

As is the case with a number of people mentioned in the Hebrews 11 Hall of Faith, I could do an entire series of chapters on the prophet Elijah. But, in the interests of space, this will be the second and final chapter on this servant of God.

In this chapter we will look at and interact with what is known as Elijah's "Power Encounter." We will see how he takes on false prophets and is victorious for the glory of God. We will also learn what the New Testament has to say about power encounters, as well as modern day power encounters and the possibility of power encounters in your life and the life of the church.

In Hebrews 11, there are hints at various power encounters. For instance, we read in *The Message* Bible of those who "were protected from lions, fires, and sword thrusts, turned disadvantage to advantage, won battles routed alien armies. Women received their loved ones back from the dead."

Or, as the New International Version puts it in the second half of verse 34, "Whose weakness was turned to strength; and who became powerful in battle and routed foreign armies."

Not every faithful person is seen as triumphing in this life, however. Here is how *The Message* puts part of that section: "there were those who, under torture, refused to give in and go free, preferring something better: resurrection. Others braved abuse and whips, and, yes, chains and dungeons." We are told that "the world didn't deserve" these people.

Let's now interact with **Elijah's power encounter** as it is faithfully reported to us in 1 Kings 18. First, we learn who the true troubler is, according to verses 17 and 18. As we learned in the previous chapter, there was a wide spread drought and famine because of King Ahab's disobedience and wickedness to the LORD God's commands.

In verse 18, Ahab twists things around and asks Elijah, "Is that you, you troubler of Israel?"

Elijah is very clear about the situation as he speaks truth to power. Here is how *The Message* has Elijah's response: "'It's not I who has caused trouble in Israel..., but you and your government--you've dumped [the LORD's] ways and commands and run off after the local Gods, the Baals.'"

The king is the true troublemaker because of his encouragement of worshiping false gods instead of the one, true, living God.

This leads to the challenge from Elijah in 1 Kings 18:19-26. Here is the challenge: bring evil Queen Jezebel's priests and have the people assemble for a power encounter.

Elijah gives the bottom line: "'How long are you going to sit on the fence? If [the LORD] is the real God, follow him; if it's Baal, follow him. Make up your minds!'"

Elijah points out that the 450 priests are outnumbered by Elijah--"the only prophet of [the LORD] left in Israel.

The people agree to Elijah's plans to recognize as the true

God whichever God brings down fire on the sacrifices.

Obviously, this is not something we are to try at home! This kind of power encounter is very rare. Below I will share a bit about power encounters in the New Testament and in our time.

But for now, let's see what happens with Elijah and his opponents. The next part of the story is the mockery from Elijah in verses 27 through 29. The priests of Baal pray all morning. They jump and stomp, but there is "not so much as a whisper of breeze."

So at noon Elijah starts "making fun of them, taunting, 'Call a little louder--he is a god, after all. Maybe he's off meditating somewhere or other, or maybe he's gotten involved in a project, or maybe he's on vacation. You don't suppose he's overslept, do you, and needs to be waked up?'"

The priests try all the harder--praying louder and louder. Then they resort to harming themselves, inflicting wounds upon themselves--as many false religions do even in our day. We read that they were "cutting themselves with swords and knives--a ritual common to them--until they were covered with blood."

We read that they "used every religious trick and strategy they knew to make something happen on the altar, but nothing happened--not so much as a whisper, not a flicker of response."

Next comes the power encounter itself in verses 30 through 38. It is vindication by and of the true God.

First, Elijah repairs the altar. It had seen better days and Elijah shows his respect for God by repairing the altar where sacrifices are to be offered in a holy way to the holy God.

Then there is reinforcement of the challenge. He has the altar covered with water and water put all around it. He ups the ante, making it even harder--from the human perspective--for God to light the sacrifice on the altar.

Elijah prays, " 'Answer me, [LORD]; O answer me and

reveal to this people that you are [the LORD], the true God, and that you are giving these people another chance at repentance.'"

Following this prayer, God honors Elijah's obedience with a rain of fire from heaven. With this power encounter, Elijah the prophet of God reaches his goal: repentance from worshiping the false god and returning to worship of the living God (see verse 39). Or, as *The Message* puts it, "All the people saw it happen and fell on their faces in awed worship, exclaiming, '[the LORD] is the true God! [The LORD] is the true God!'"

By their acknowledgment that the LORD is the true God, they are repenting--turning from the false God Baal and turning to the true God. They are changing their mind both about Baal and about the LORD.

When the goal is achieved, there are also consequences. First come the negative consequences for the false prophets in verse 40.

Next come the positive consequences. The whole point of the drought was Ahab (and Jezebel's) disobedience to the LORD by following and worshiping a false prophet. Because the people have repented and worshiped the LORD, the curse is lifted.

We read about this in verses 41 through 46. *The Message* puts verse 45 this way, "Things happened fast. The sky grew black with wind-driven clouds, and then a huge cloudburst of rain, with Ahab hightailing it in his chariot for Jezreel."

Let's look now at **what the New Testament and Modern Day experience have to say about power encounters.** In the Bible they are called miracles. They are also called signs and wonders.

As the writer of the Book of Hebrews puts it in 4:3&4: "How shall we escape if we ignore such a great salvation? This salvation, which was first announced by the LORD, was confirmed to us by those who heard him. God also testified to it by signs, wonders and various miracles, and gifts of the Holy Spirit distributed according to his will."

Of course, Jesus had power encounters while on earth. In Luke 11:14-23 we read how Jesus faces down the messengers of evil --the Devil's slaves known as demons. In verse 20 He says, "If I drive out [or cast out] demons by the finger of God, then the Kingdom of God has come to you."

These power encounters continue in the Book of Acts, where we see the birth and growth of the Church in the Roman Empire and beyond. I will give you only two examples of power encounters.

One has to do with a curse, like Elijah placed on Israel due to Ahab's disobedience to God. In Acts 13 we meet Elymas the sorcerer who opposed the Christian faith by trying to turn the Roman leader from the faith.

Starting in verse nine we read that "Saul [or Paul], full of the Holy Spirit and looking him straight in the eye, said, 'You bag of wind, you parody of a devil--why, you stay up nights inventing schemes to cheat people out of God. But now you've come up against God himself, and your game is up. You're about to go blind--no sunlight for you for a good long stretch.' He was plunged immediately into a shadowy mist and stumbled around, begging people to take his hand and show him the way."

When the Roman ruler "saw what happened, he became a believer, full of enthusiasm over what they were saying about the" LORD. So even in what might be viewed as a negative power encounter, God was glorified and the faith of an individual was strengthened.

That is what power encounters are all about--the glory and worship of God. Do you remember what the Israelites did after the power encounter with Elijah and the false prophets? They worshiped the LORD.

The second example of power encounter for Kingdom work

has to do with an unmitigated blessing.   At the beginning of Acts 3 we read that Peter and John are on their way to the temple for a prayer meeting.   A crippled man is being carried to a gate of the Jewish Temple.

The cripple looks at the two men, hoping they will give him some money.   I like how the King James Version puts it--these words have even been put into a song: "Silver and gold have I none.   But what I have I give unto you--in the Name of Jesus Christ, get up and walk!"

The man goes into the temple, "Walking back and forth, dancing and praising God.   Everybody there saw him walking around and praising God."

This was all for God's glory.   That is what power encounters are all about--not for the glorification of Peter or Paul or anyone else.

We also read about power encounters in the letters of Paul. In 2 Corinthians 12:12 Paul refers to them to prove to a resistant church--one he started!--that he is a genuine apostle: "All the signs that mark a true apostle were in evidence while I was with you through both good times and bad: signs of portent, signs of wonder, signs of power."

The reality of signs and wonders is seen throughout church history and down to the present day.   John Wimber first spoke of "signs and wonders" in a message at Fuller Theological Seminary in 1981.   It is a controversial issue these days.

But he has written a challenging book along with Kevin Springer entitled *Power Encounters among Christians in the Western World*.   With those last two words we see that God breaking into space and time with His power and for His glory is not confined to some when back in time or somewhere overseas.

But I did find a true story of a modern day power encounter in Africa.   I found it at 4thrugh.net.   "One missionary from the

International Mission Board of the Southern Baptist Convention had a very exciting and powerful experience. He was sent to a large Muslim city in Africa to find ways to win the people to the Lord.

"His love and compassion for them was apparent to all, and in a short time he gained the friendship and respect of many Muslims in the city. One day he received a telephone call from the eighty-year-old Imam, the leader of the central mosque, who asked if he would come to their mosque and bless his people in the name of Jesus.

"At the meeting, the Imam asked the missionary to pray for his people, and after praying for some in the mosque, a distinguished looking man stood up and brought his eight-year-old daughter to the front, asking the missionary to pray that God would heal her withered legs. The father heard that there was 'power in the name of Jesus.'

"Immediately after the prayer, the condition of the girl remained unchanged. The father thanked the missionary and returned to the back of the mosque. The girl struggled in her father's arms until he put her down and she stood on her legs for the first time in her life. She had been healed.

"After this power encounter, many Muslims in that area of Africa believed and were converted to Christianity, not because of an intellectual change but because of a real spiritual power encounter."

Power encounters certainly have their place in evangelism. As we have seen in Elijah's time, they also serve to bring people back to worship of the true and living God.

With that, I turn now to **the church and you**. I wrote earlier that Wimber's book shows that power encounters today are not confined to the cutting edge of missions overseas. They are happening in the United States and probably even in the state where you live.

I do want to give a caution here. There can be counterfeit spiritual happenings as well. But Jesus also addresses that in Luke 11. He points out that He drives out demons by the finger of God, not by Beelzebub--which is another name for Baal which is another name for Satan or the Devil. The kingdom of Satan cannot stand. Meanwhile, the Kingdom of God is going from strength to strength, even in the midst of persecution.

What does all this power encounter stuff have to do with you? Well, first of all, is your view of the universe open enough to be willing to accept the possibility of God doing a power encounter in your church and in your life?

It can be a pretty scary thing, but the outcome is for the glory of God. I am sure you do not want to experience a power encounter in the form of a curse because of disobedience to God or worshiping a false God such as a person or money or fame or security or perfect health, or--you fill in the blank.

I hope you will be open to the possibility of God doing one or more power encounters through your church in the form of a blessing for worshiping the true God and for drawing others to Himself.

There was a time when I first arrived in a community when God chose to promptly answer several prayers for a person's family. The person found it almost scary at how quickly and well the prayers were answered. I do not take any credit for that. God chose to answer those prayers in that way at that time.

But getting back to you and your church. Do you remember the pattern of Elijah? First, he

Repaired the altar. What is it in your church that needs to be repaired? Of course there are the ongoing repairs of the physical structure.

But is there also the need to repair relationships and

attitudes? Is there someone with whom you need to work through something? Jesus tells us we are to make peace with others before we bring our offerings to the altar.

And how about attitudes? Are we choosing to look at looming challenges rather than praise and trust the God in Whom all things are possible? Yes, we face the challenges square in the eye, but we do so with both eyes on Jesus, obeying what He says about the matter and moving forward for His Kingdom. There is repair. There is also

*Reinforcement

of what God wants of us. He wants us individually to read the Bible and pray. He wants us to serve and give. But we are better together. He wants us in small group Bible study and prayer groups. He wants us to serve together and pull together in giving.

All of this reinforces our trust and following God. There is repair and reinforcement. Then comes

*God's Refiner's Fire

through renewal and revival. When this happens there is repentance and worship.

Some people in some churches are praying for revival locally, nationally and globally. Will you join with them? Will you open yourself to the refiner's fire in your heart that leads to repentance and new life in Christ?

Maybe the first power encounter you need is with the living God yourself. To receive His power within you to energize you to worship Him, serve others and seek His glory in all that you say and do!

"Revive us again--fill each heart with Thy love;

May each soul be rekindled with fire from above.

Hallelujah, Thine the glory! Hallelujah, Amen!

Hallelujah, Thine the Glory! *Revive us again!* "

- Section 28 -

Daniel: "What Do You See?"

"O king, live forever!" said Daniel. "My God sent his angel, who closed the mouths of the lions so that they would not hurt me. I've been found innocent before God and also before you, O king. I've done nothing to harm you."
Daniel 6 The Message

Have you ever watched T.V. preachers?   They come in all kinds of sizes and abilities.   When I was recovering from surgery, David Jeremiah was a great encouragement to me.   He is on when I usually am at church.

Someone who is on earlier is Charles Stanley.   On one Sunday I happened to catch a short yet powerful devotional message by him as I was getting ready to go to church.

Stanley stood in front of a mural of Daniel in the lion's den and told the following true story: many years ago he was having significant difficulty in the church that he was serving.

An elderly member of the church heard that he was going through a hard time and invited him over to her home.   She showed him a picture of Daniel in the lion's den.

She asked Dr. Stanley, "What do you see?"   He described the picture as well as he could.   But she was not satisfied with his answer and asked him again, "Please tell me, what do you see?"

Finally she gave him the answer she was looking for: "Daniel is not looking at the lions!"   In other words, he was looking up at the glory of God, trusting God to take care of the situation.

This picture and conversation had such an impact on Dr. Stanley that he eventually had a large mural made of the picture. I hope that the true story of Daniel in the lion's den has a similar

195

impact on you as you read this chapter as I ask, "What do you see?"

I will be asking that question of the various people involved in the situation of Daniel six. First let's take a look at the bureaucrats. **What do the bureaucrats see?**

First, I would like to write a few words about bureaucrats. The word has a negative connotation about government officials who are not helpful to the ordinary citizen.

That can be the case in our time, but I will tell you that I have experienced a number of helpful government officials. A U.S. embassy official in another country was a great help to me at one point.

When I worked for a congresswoman in 2003, any number of federal officials were of great help---whether it was helping straighten out Social Security snafus or helping return two abducted daughters to their father, government officials were of great help.

But the bureaucrats in Daniel 6 regrettably fit the stereotype of being unhelpful and in it for themselves. They want power for power's sake.

We read in Daniel six--according to *The Message*--that "Daniel, brimming with spirit and intelligence, so completely outclassed the other vice-regents and governors that the king decided to put him in charge of the whole kingdom."

This leads to jealousy against Daniel. The bureaucrats look at Daniel and see a threat. Instead of turning to God or at least recognizing that they should serve the people and not their own self-interest, they look at Daniel and his abilities and see a threat.

They meet and try to find a skeleton in his closet. But they realize he is a man of integrity, who is "totally exemplary and trustworthy. They could find no evidence of negligence or misconduct."

So they decide, "We're never going to find anything against

this Daniel unless we can cook up something religious."

They turn to what is at the center of Daniel's being--his core of integrity of worship of the one living and true God. They decide to twist that against him and act deceptively.

They bring a decree to the king. They trick the king. They flatter him and get him to agree to an irrevocable law that for thirty days people are to pray only to the king, under the penalty of being thrown into the lions' den.

They play upon the king's pride and do not mention Daniel and his faith. Which leads us to the second major question, namely **what does the king see?** Sadly, the king does *not* see the hidden agenda of the bureaucrats. Sometimes we are so blinded by our own ambition, hopes or dreams that we do not see that the people trying to get us to do something are doing it for themselves, for their own hidden agenda.

I don't know how many junk e-mails I have received that tell me I have won a lottery I never entered--be it in England, Malaysia or somewhere else.

And then there were the recurring emails from the fictitious Mrs. Mary Williams of Nigeria who told me that she was dying and wanted me to have her late husband's millions to use for Christian purposes.

Of course we know that all of these are scams to get our personal financial information to and to rob us blind.

What the bureaucrats are doing here is attempting to rob the king of his closest and best adviser. By giving in to his own overblown view of himself, the king apparently seals Daniel's doom.

Once the king learns of the implications of what he has done, he sees himself in a painful, complicated situation. He tries to wiggle out of what he has done, but the bureaucrats gleefully remind him, "'Remember, O king, it's the law of the Medes and

Persians that the king's decree can never be changed.'"

And so we read that "the king caved in and ordered Daniel brought and thrown into the lions' den."

The king will see that the true God works mightily. Most of that will come later. But before Daniel is taken to the lions he says to Daniel, "'Your God, to whom you are so loyal, is going to get you out of this.'"

He knows enough about Daniel's God that he can be saved even from this situation. In the meantime, the king does not eat. He does not sleep. He fasts and prays for Daniel during the night.

Jesus says, "When you fast" not "if you fast." Now, some people have medical conditions that preclude them from fasting from food. You can have a partial fast. Or fast from something else, such as T.V. or social media.

Jesus talks about the importance of combining prayer with fasting. At any rate, King Darius--king of the greatest empire of the time--prays and fasts for Daniel during the night Daniel is in the lions' den.

Which leads us to the third major question: **What does Daniel see?** By introduction, I can tell you that Daniel sees the way of obedience after the terrible decree is issued. We read that "when Daniel learned that the decree had been signed and posted, he continued to pray just as he had always done."

"The conspirators came and found him praying, asking God for help. They went straight to the king and reminded him of the royal decree that he had signed."

So the king "sealed the cover with his signet ring and the signet rings of all his nobles, fixing Daniels' fate," as people supposed.

But, what does Daniel see in the lion's den? I can tell you he does *not* look at the lions, be it the treacherous dealing of the bureaucrats or the literal lions who appear to mean imminent death.

When it comes to the lions

*of treachery, Daniel had gone about his prayer business, obeying God rather than men. He knew what the men were up to, but he had an audience of One--God, to whom he prayed and in whom he put his trust.

Once in the lions' den, he does not look at the lions

*of imminent death. He is in the den. He knows the very hungry lions are there. But that is where the picture that means so much to Charles Stanley comes in.

He sees God. Daniel is looking to God. Daniel sees God's glory and knows everything will be alright. The Bible is silent as to the specifics, the "how" of what happens in the den, but it is clear that God takes care of the lions.

At the break of day, the king rushes to the lions' den. He approaches the den and calls out anxiously, "Daniel, servant of the living God, has your God, whom you serve so loyally, saved you from the lions?"

Daniel responds and with his first word makes it clear to the king that, indeed, the living God Whom he serves has saved him from the lions: "O king, live forever!" ..."My God sent his angel, who closed the mouths of the lions so that they would not hurt me. I've been found innocent before God and also before you, O king. I've done nothing to harm you."

The king is relieved and happy that Daniel is alive and unharmed. Next, the king exercises his authority and has the bureaucrats thrown to the lions, who tear them to pieces before they hit the floor.

The chapter concludes with the king proclaiming the glories of the living God, based on what he--and Daniel--have seen. He sends a proclamation to everyone in his empire, a proclamation that says:

"Peace to you!   Abundant peace!

I decree that Daniel's God shall be worshiped and feared in all parts of my kingdom.

He is the living God, world without end.   His kingdom never falls.   His rule continues eternally.

He is the Savior and Rescuer.

He performs astonishing miracles in heaven and on earth.

He saved Daniel from the power of the lions."

We also read that Daniel was restored to his position. "From then on, Daniel was treated well during the reign of Darius, and also in the following reign of Cyrus the Persian."

When it comes to "Daniel in the lions' den, we have seen what the bureaucrats see; what the king sees; and what Daniel sees. Now, as we come to direct application of this text, I ask the most important question: **What do _you_ see?**

What are the lions in your life?   What are the challenges that seem so great that they threaten to tear you apart?   Is your obedience to God causing you to be unjustly accused and punished?

I encourage you to bring your "lions" before the LORD. Talk with Him frankly about them.   Search the Scriptures for His guidance, remembering that obedience to God is always His will for you.

Sometimes the obedience is clear, such as the Ten Commandments, the Beatitudes, or the other commandments of Jesus.   Jesus says, "If you love me, you will keep my commandments."

The Book of Proverbs shows the way to true wisdom--"The fear of the Lord," rather than the fear of lions.   The Book of James characterizes the devil as a lion prowling around seeking whom he may devour.

Christ is your wisdom in difficult circumstances. Christ is your peace in the midst of turmoil.

I once read a novel about a young woman who goes to Los Angeles to become an attorney. It is called *City of Angels* and is the first in the Shannon Saga, as in Kathleen "Kit" Shannon.

After her arrival in Los Angeles, she faces a number of major challenges, or lions if you will. At one point, when the opposition becomes so intense--even from a relative--she takes out her late father's Bible. She reads it for "devotion and direction. Papa had taught her that Scripture always came first when seeking God's will."

May that be the case for you as well. May you be like Daniel, who sees the God who will deliver him.

What each one of us needs is *vision*. I wrote at the beginning of this chapter the picture of Daniel in the lions' den. I told you about the question the elderly member of the church asked Dr. Stanley: "What do you see?"

After I thought about that story for a couple of days, God gave me a song about it. I wrote down the words and then a friend wrote down the music to go with it. It is called "What do you see?" Here are the lyrics:

The Refrain is God speaking to us:

"What do you see?

Tell me, what do you see?"

Each verse is short:

I see Daniel in the lion's den.

I see a cave dark and bleak.

Refrain

I see stones on the walls,
I see lions by his side.

Refrain

I see Daniel in the den,
I see no way out.
Lord, what do you see?

The rest of the song is God's response to that question.

"I see Daniel standing there,
Looking up at me.
He beholds my glory.

"I see Daniel looking at
The Stone that was rejected.
I see him looking at the Lion of Judah."

The song concludes with God asking each of us the question:

"Do you see... me?"

That song and Daniel's experience is about vision. May it be the case with us--may the LORD of our hearts be our vision as we move forward with Him, not looking at the lions, but looking at Him.

"Be Thou my vision, O Lord of my heart;

Nought be all else to me save that Thou art.
Thou my best thought, by day or by night,
Waking or sleeping, Thy presence my light."

- Section 29 -

REFLECTION BENCH

Not one of these people, even though their lives of faith were exemplary, got their hands on what was promised. God had a better plan for us: that their faith and our faith would come together to make one completed whole, their lives of faith not complete apart from ours.
Hebrews 11:39&40   The Message

In this chapter we arrive at a transitional location on the Hall of Faith grounds.   We have made it all the way through the building that provides us with a definition of faith, the reality of God the Creator, and introduces us to faithful people found in what we now call the Old Testament.

Most recently we have been in the Gallery of Faithful People.   We arrive now at one end of that Gallery and find a bench. It is called the Reflection Bench.

Here we sit to reflect on what we have learned about what it means to be a person of faith--- the examples of people's lives, the faith we saw at work in so many of life's different situations.

In the Gallery of Faithful People we have seen people by faith overcome great obstacles and opposition.   There is deliverance, conquest and new life.

But we notice something different about the Reflection Bench.   It is in the shape of a cross.   That is an indication to us of two things.   First, being faithful often involves suffering.   The Bible tells us that "all who would live a godly life in Christ Jesus will suffer."

A T. V. preacher once said that the doctrine that Christians must suffer is "straight from the pit of hell."   Well, because of what the Bible says about suffering, I am afraid that the reverse is true and he needs to reconsider what he said.

The second indication we receive from the Reflection Bench

is that the faithful people who suffered before the time of Christ were commended for their faith, yet were not fulfilled until Christ went to the cross.

In the last part of verses 35 through 38, we are reminded that, more often than not, **suffering** is the lot of God's faithful people. The author discusses different kind of suffering which people underwent before our Redeemer arrived on the scene.

Imprisonment and torture are described. The word for torture has to do with being stretched on a rack and tortured to death.

The prophet Jeremiah experienced several of the afflictions described here. He was beaten and put into stocks. He became a laughingstock. Finally, tradition has it, he was stoned by the people he was in exile with because they could not stand his preaching against their idolatry.

Death has sometimes been the earthly end of those putting God before all else. It is said that the prophet Isaiah was sawn in two. In the early days of the Church, Herod Agrippa killed James the brother of John with the sword. But when he tried to do the same to Peter, God provided a way of escape. But, years later Peter would be crucified upside down in Rome.

The point is that we live and die by faith. "By faith one lived, and by faith the other died." All looked forward to what is called "a better resurrection."

You might remember the true story I told from the Bible in a recent chapter about Elijah returning the widow's son to life. Jesus also raised Lazarus from the dead and the son of a widow in a village called Nain.

I have news for you. Each of them eventually died, was put in the grave, and stayed there.

The better resurrection is that which brings about never ending life in the presence of Jesus. That is what faithful people were--and are--looking forward to. Through the ages, some have been imprisoned, others were killed.

Many, many suffered deprivation. We read of that in Hebrews 11:37&38. Because of their faithfulness, they are deprived of all but the meanest clothing and housing.

The reference here is probably to "those godly Jews [in the first century before Christ] who fled from the persecution under Antiochus Epiphanes," one of the cruelest rulers who ever lived.

Persecution continues to this day in various parts of the world. One organization called Voice of the Martyrs documents this persecution through a regular publication and in other ways. In this material and from some other organizations we learn of very real challenges to individual Christians and churches in one country or another.

The faithful have suffered much through the generations and down the centuries. But each has discovered a secret. That is how faith transforms us in the midst of suffering. Faith recognizes that God "is on the throne of the universe." "Faith recognizes that everything [that] enters our lives is ordered by Him Who is our Father, and that our enemies can do nothing whatever against us without His direct permission."

"Faith recognizes that our enemies' malicious efforts will be made to work together for our good." "By mixing itself with God's promises, faith obtains present help, strength and consolation from God."

"Faith looks away from the present conflict, and views the promised rest." "It is the fiery trial [that] puts to the test the kind of faith we really possess." The faithful people spoken of in Hebrews 11 had the right stuff.

Faith which---according to verse 39---is worthy of commendation. Remember Hebrews 11:2. Referring to the operative definition of faith in verse one, it says "this is what the ancients were commended for." So, we have come full circle.

Why are the "ancients" commended? "Because of their

trusting in Christ alone for salvation, and because of their walking in obedience to His revealed will, they received" approval. Hebrews 11--the Hall of Faith--looks back to the stars, the heroes, the martyrs of faith before the days of Jesus.

But the writer is not on a nostalgia trip. He has a very definite purpose in what he writes.

His emphasis, his goal--as seen in verses 39&40--is to help his listeners to realize that **the best is yet to come!** "These were all commended for their faith, yet none of them received what had been promised. God had planned something better for us so that only together with us would they be made perfect."

What is the promise? It is singular, not plural--promise, not promises. The implication is that "some pre-eminent excellent thing [is promised] and this is Jesus Christ, the Divine Savior."

"The Old Testament saints did not live to see historically accomplished that which their faith specifically embraced."

Jesus speaks of this to his disciples: "Blessed are your eyes because they see, and your ears because they hear. For I tell you the truth, many prophets and righteous men longed to see what you see but did not see it, and to hear what you hear but did not hear it."

Peter writes about the same thing in his first letter: "Concerning this salvation, the prophets, who spoke of the grace that was to come to you, searched intently and with the greatest care, trying to find out the time and circumstances to which the Spirit of Christ in them was pointing when he predicted the sufferings of Christ and the glories that would follow. It was revealed to them that they were not serving themselves but you, when they spoke of the things that have now been told you by those who have preached the Gospel to you by the Holy Spirit sent from heaven. Even angels long to look into these things."

What is it that the angels long to look into? The better way, the new covenant that brings the faithful of old to completion.

"The 'better plan' [that] God has made embraces the better hope, the better promise, the better covenant, the better sacrifices, the better and abiding possessions, and the better resurrection [that] is their heritage and ours."

We have had a long sit on the Meditation Bench, which is in the shape of the cross. We have considered the suffering and commendation that the faithful have received.

They have been persecuted by the world. "They were outlawed as people who were unfit for civilized society: the truth was that civilized society was unfit for them."

As the writer of Hebrews puts it, "The world was not worthy of them." But they were worthy of commendation, approval from God.

We may join with them, rejoicing that Christ has come, will come again, and that, therefore, the best is yet to come.

As Charles Wesley writes in a hymn,
"E'en now by faith we join our hands
    With those that went before
And greet the blood-be-sprinkled hands
    On the eternal shore."

As I think about that hymn and some of the martyrs of the faith and think about the cross-shaped Meditation Bench and the Lord's Supper, I am reminded of Paul's words in Philippians 3:10&11 where he writes, "I want to know Christ and the power of his resurrection and the fellowship of sharing in his sufferings, becoming like him in his death, and so, somehow, to attain to the resurrection from the dead."

We come to the resurrection through suffering. Our suffering does not save us. Paul's suffering does not save us. Only Jesus' suffering and dying on the cross saves us--when we receive that work for ourselves.

As we sit upon the reflection bench, we have considered all

that has gone before.   But we also look forward.   We look down a long hall way.   We stand up and walk toward a very significant part of the Hall of Faith.

THE STADIUM

- Section 30 -

"In the Arena/Great Cloud of Witnesses"

Do you see what this means--all these pioneers who blazed the way, all these veterans cheering us on? It means we'd better get on with it. Strip down, start running--and never quit! No extra spiritual fat, no parasitic sins.
Hebrews 12:1   The Message

[Author's note: I originally planned on one chapter. With the 2008 150th anniversary celebration of First Congregational Church of Charles City, I have divided the concluding three verses into two chapters.]

A football stadium stands near the NFL Hall of Fame complex. Each year--after the most recently elected people are inducted into the Hall of Fame--the first preseason football game of the year is played in that stadium.

The game of football is intended to be played, not merely discussed or watched. You can have all the cheer leaders and exciting jumbotron action, but it is meaningless unless the game is played.

Similarly, while on earth we need to be participants not spectators. Inspired by those who have gone before--both in the Old Testament and throughout the church age of 2000 years--we walk down the corridor and approach the stadium.

This reminds me of the first time I attended a Rose Bowl game. It was January 1, 1972, and Stanford was set to play Michigan. The friends taking my family left a bit late from their San Marino home and therefore we arrived in our chauffeur-driven

211

car after the game had begun. We were dropped off just outside the stadium, under the large rose.

Even though the game had already begun, I could hear nothing outside of the stadium. As I walked through a tunnel that took me inside the stadium, the roar of the crowd gradually increased to deafening proportions.

The game was on and it was exciting! The athletes were being cheered on by their fans, their partisans.

Similarly, as you walk down the tunnel from the reflection bench, you begin to hear the roar of the crowd. This time, however, the cheering is completely one-sided. It is for you!

The crowd is the "great cloud of witnesses" mentioned in the first verse of Hebrews 12. These are the ones who have gone before in faith. Do you see them, from the Old Testament? Do you see the greats and the unknowns (but fully known and loved by God) of Church history? Martyrs for the faith and those who died at a full age--who finished well in their faith.

They are cheering you on! As you take steps of faith onto the floor, the track of the arena, these every day saints are cheering you on as you move forward in your life of faith.

It is at this point that we need to heed the words given us by the author of Hebrews in verse one of chapter 12. We have already spoken of being surrounded by the great cloud of witnesses. Next we are told what it takes to run the race of faith: "let us throw off everything that hinders and the sin that so easily entangles, and let us run with perseverance the race marked out for us."

In 12:1 we realize that we are surrounded by **a great cloud of witnesses**, a host of God's faithful people who have already completed and run the race. These people are witnesses in two ways.

First, they are witnesses to the faithfulness of God. During their lifetime "they have borne witness to the faithfulness of God." "By their love and endurance they have borne witness to the possibilities of the life of faith."

The second way that these people of faith are witnesses is that they are witnesses to us. They are an encouragement to us when the life of faith is tough.

This cloud of witnesses, this host of faithful people is an encouragement to us, a motivating force. We *do* need encouragement and motivation sometimes, don't we?

It is true that we as Christians "have greater incentives and fuller encouragement than any of our predecessors who lived before Christ came, but we too have our race to run."

We are in the arena and **running the race**. There are impediments that can keep runners from racing at their best. There are hindrances. The athlete must get rid of all extra weight, not only of heavy objects carried on the body, but also excesses bodily weight.

There are entanglements. Sometimes the best of athletes might trip coming out of the starting blocks. I do not know if you remember all the way back to the 1984 Olympics in Los Angeles.

Vividly etched in my memory when I think of entanglements is the tragic occurrence of Zola Budd tripping Mary Decker. The rage, disappointment, everything etched on Decker's face.

There are hindrances in the lives of Christians trying to run the race of faith. There is the weight of worry, or of not feeling up to the task to which God has called us. You might think "I'm too young" or "I'm too old." These are not sins, but they are weights that hinder our progress.

Then there is that which is flat out sin and causes us to stumble when we have just begun. We are to run with perseverance the race marked out for us. A marathon is in view here. The course of any marathon is marked out in the streets. It requires perseverance--getting through what is called "the wall"-- keeping on even when your body cries out to stop.

To every Olympic marathoner who makes it, there is the joy of entering the stadium and hearing the roar of the crowd for the final lap.

We are engaged in the marathon of life. We are not talking here about a sprint. The course is marked out for us in the Word of God. Endurance is required. There is a need for spiritual fitness and awareness. A major tip on how to be fit and aware is found in the first part of verse two.

We are to be fixing our eyes on Jesus, as I will focus on in the next chapter.

For now, let's resolve to be in the arena, running the race that is set before us. Let us be encouraged by the great cloud of witnesses who are cheering us on.

They are called saints, not because of any value in themselves but because they exercised the gift of faith God gave them to do great things for God. In the Old Testament, New Testament, and Church history--including the history of your church--God has enabled extraordinary people to do extraordinary things for His glory!

In the lead up to First Congregational's 150th anniversary, a reporter asked me how it was that the church had lasted 150 years. My response was, "God's faithfulness." I talked about the fact that God had and has a purpose for that church--as the bylaws say--"to propagate the Gospel and advance the Kingdom of God."

Let's remember the faithful people, the witnesses, the saints of your church and in the centuries past.

"For all the saints, who from their labors rest,

Who Thee by faith before the world confessed,

214

Thy Name, O Jesus, be forever blest.

"O May Thy soldiers, faithful, true, and bold,
Fight as the saints who nobly fought of old,
And with them the victor's crown of gold.
Alleluia!"

- Section 31 -

"Fixing Our Eyes on Jesus"

Keep your eyes on Jesus, who both began and finished this race we're in. Study how he did it. Because he never lost sight of where he was headed--that exhilarating finish in and with God--he could put up with anything along the way: cross, shame, whatever. And now he's there, in the place of honor, right alongside God. When you find yourselves flagging in your faith, go over that story again, item by item, that long litany of hostility he plowed through. That will shoot adrenaline into your souls!

Hebrews 1:2&3

I have a friend who lives west of the Mississippi. When we met he was the main owner of a professional baseball team. Since then, his brother has taken the lead. I continue to stay in touch with the first brother through email. One year the team had an exhilarating run in September and October.

In September the team came from way behind to tie for the wild card position and then conquered through the playoffs until they came to the World Series. During this period (mainly during the playoffs) I sent my friend a short devotional via e-mail almost every day.

One day I wanted to make sure that he was keeping things in perspective and that he was keeping his focus on the right thing, or Person--Jesus Christ. So I wrote him about the above verse and said I hoped he was fixing his eyes on Jesus. He wrote me back the following: "Totally fixated on Him."

The team was as focused on their mission as the owner was focused on Jesus. Every athlete knows the importance of being focused.

For the Christian what, or *Whom*, we focus on is even more

217

important. **Our focus must be upon Jesus.** That is the whole point of Hebrews 11--of the "Hall of Faith"---to turn our eyes, our full attention to Jesus.

Who is this Jesus on Whom we are to focus? He is the Author and Perfecter of our faith. Jesus is presented here as "the one who has blazed the trail of faith and as the one who Himself ran the race of faith to its triumphant finish."

"'Author and Finisher' or 'Captain and Completer' means Jesus is beyond all comparison." We now know something of Who Jesus is.

I next ask **what has Jesus done for us?** He has set an example by being focused on obedience to the will of His heavenly Father.

He has set us an example by keeping in mind the joy of the goal. When I think of being focused and having a goal, I remember a scene from the movie "Chariots of Fire." The Jewish athlete Harold Abrahams is preparing to run a sprint at the 1924 Paris Olympic Summer Games. The camera shows the scene from his eyes. There is light on one lane--his. There is one goal--the finish line. You see and hear nothing else except the sound of cleats scratching in the dirt. Harold Abrahams was focused on running the race and the goal before him.

Jesus has set an example for us by focusing on the joy of the goal. He has *died* for us. He has *endured* the cross. He has *scorned* the shame of the cross and it *was* a shameful way to die.   In the Roman world, "to die by crucifixion was to plumb the lowest depths of disgrace; it was a punishment reserved for those who were deemed of all men most unfit to live."

Jesus has risen and ascended for us. He has sat down at the right hand of God. Hebrews 2:9 speaks eloquently to us at this point, "But we see Jesus, who was made a little lower than the angels, now crowned with glory and honor because he suffered death, so that by the grace of God he might taste death for everyone."

I once had the privilege of visiting the Coliseum in Rome--where gladiators, lions and Christians, among others, had met. Christians had been slain for their faith. I was overcome with awe and wonder when, after coming through the tunnel and walking as far toward the field as was allowed, I discovered that on the place where the Emperor had given the thumbs up or thumbs down--signaling life or death--there now stands a cross.

At the cross, Jesus received the thumbs down from Pilate. But we know, from the perspective of Resurrection Day, that at the cross, *in Christ*, we have received the thumbs up.

That is why the writer of the letter to the Hebrews--those early Jewish Christians undergoing persecution and wondering whether they should chuck their Christian faith--**calls for a consideration of Jesus.** Consider Jesus, who endured opposition from sinful men. There is that word again: endurance. Jesus endured opposition and so will any Christian who takes his or her LORD seriously. We are in mortal combat.

We are to consider what Jesus went through so that we do not grow weary and lose heart. Even the best of athletes gets tired and experiences times of discouragement. It is *how* we deal with those times that is important.

I do not believe it is a coincidence that some of our best athletes were also in the military--Roger Staubach (football) and David Robinson (basketball), some boxers, and others come to mind. They know the importance of discipline, fitness and focusing on the objective.

When we as Christians become tired and discouraged, where are we to turn? "When we become weary on the way, and grow faint at heart because there seems no end to the trials we have to endure, let us consider Jesus."

"'*Consider Him'*: *there* is the remedy against faintness of mind; *there* is the preservation from such 'weariness" of dejection'... that we are ready to throw down our weapons and throw up our hands in despair.   It is the diligent consideration of the person of Christ, the Object of faith, the Supporter of faith."

Every time summer Olympic Games are held, you will see athletes and coaches representing over 200 nations walking into the stadium for the opening ceremonies. In the weeks that follow you watch some of the competition--it is exciting, agonizing, inspiring.

The athletes will be in various arenas and at various venues. They are competing for their countries and themselves.   The winners will receive gold medals.

Whenever you watch these games, I hope you will remember that you are in an arena--the arena of life.   You are not playing a game, but for keeps.

You are being rooted on by a cloud, a host of witnesses, though it is "not so much they who look at us as we who look to them--for encouragement."

As you remember them and their putting their faith into action, I hope you will:
*set aside your sin;
*fix your eyes on Jesus,
*see the Lord of lords--your Captain--giving you the thumbs up;
*and endure the opposition for the joy that is set before you!

"Turn your eyes upon Jesus.
Look full on His wonderful face.
And the things of earth will grow strangely dim
In the light of His glory and grace."